ISBN 0-8373-4133-7
C-4133   **CAREER EXAMINATION SERIES**

This is your PASSBOOK® for...

Sign Electrician

Test Preparation Study Guide
Questions & Answers

NATIONAL LEARNING CORPORATION®

PASSBOOK®
NOTICE

PASSBOOK SERIES®

THE *PASSBOOK SERIES®* has been created to prepare applicants and candidates for the ultimate academic battlefield – the examination room.

At some time in our lives, each and every one of us may be required to take an examination – for validation, matriculation, admission, qualification, registration, certification, or licensure.

Based on the assumption that every applicant or candidate has met the basic formal educational standards, has taken the required number of courses, and read the necessary texts, the *PASSBOOK SERIES®* furnishes the one special preparation which may assure passing with confidence, instead of failing with insecurity. Examination questions – together with answers – are furnished as the basic vehicle for study so that the mysteries of the examination and its compounding difficulties may be eliminated or diminished by a sure method.

This book is meant to help you pass your examination provided that you qualify and are serious in your objective.

The entire field is reviewed through the huge store of content information which is succinctly presented through a provocative and challenging approach – the question-and-answer method.

A climate of success is established by furnishing the correct answers at the end of each test.

You soon learn to recognize types of questions, forms of questions, and patterns of questioning. You may even begin to anticipate expected outcomes.

You perceive that many questions are repeated or adapted so that you can gain acute insights, which may enable you to score many sure points.

You learn how to confront new questions, or types of questions, and to attack them confidently and work out the correct answers.

You note objectives and emphases, and recognize pitfalls and dangers, so that you may make positive educational adjustments.

Moreover, you are kept fully informed in relation to new concepts, methods, practices, and directions in the field.

You discover that you are actually taking the examination all the time: you are preparing for the examination by "taking" an examination, not by reading extraneous and/or supererogatory textbooks.

In short, this PASSBOOK®, used directedly, should be an important factor in helping you to pass your test.

SIGN ELECTRICIAN

DUTIES
Electrifies, installs and repairs outdoor electric signs. Performs related duties.

SCOPE OF THE EXAMINATION
The written test will cover knowledge, skills, and/or abilities in such areas as:
1. Definitions, calculations, theory and plans;
2. Electrical services, service equipment and separately derived systems;
3. Electrical feeders;
4. Branch circuit calculations and conductors;
5. Electrical wiring methods and electrical materials;
6. Electrical equipment and devices; and
7. Motors;
8. Electrical control devices and disconnecting means; and
9. Electric signs and outline lighting.

HOW TO TAKE A TEST

I. YOU MUST PASS AN EXAMINATION

A. WHAT EVERY CANDIDATE SHOULD KNOW

Examination applicants often ask us for help in preparing for the written test. What can I study in advance? What kinds of questions will be asked? How will the test be given? How will the papers be graded?

As an applicant for a civil service examination, you may be wondering about some of these things. Our purpose here is to suggest effective methods of advance study and to describe civil service examinations.

Your chances for success on this examination can be increased if you know how to prepare. Those "pre-examination jitters" can be reduced if you know what to expect. You can even experience an adventure in good citizenship if you know why civil service exams are given.

B. WHY ARE CIVIL SERVICE EXAMINATIONS GIVEN?

Civil service examinations are important to you in two ways. As a citizen, you want public jobs filled by employees who know how to do their work. As a job seeker, you want a fair chance to compete for that job on an equal footing with other candidates. The best-known means of accomplishing this two-fold goal is the competitive examination.

Exams are widely publicized throughout the nation. They may be administered for jobs in federal, state, city, municipal, town or village governments or agencies.

Any citizen may apply, with some limitations, such as the age or residence of applicants. Your experience and education may be reviewed to see whether you meet the requirements for the particular examination. When these requirements exist, they are reasonable and applied consistently to all applicants. Thus, a competitive examination may cause you some uneasiness now, but it is your privilege and safeguard.

C. HOW ARE CIVIL SERVICE EXAMS DEVELOPED?

Examinations are carefully written by trained technicians who are specialists in the field known as "psychological measurement," in consultation with recognized authorities in the field of work that the test will cover. These experts recommend the subject matter areas or skills to be tested; only those knowledges or skills important to your success on the job are included. The most reliable books and source materials available are used as references. Together, the experts and technicians judge the difficulty level of the questions.

Test technicians know how to phrase questions so that the problem is clearly stated. Their ethics do not permit "trick" or "catch" questions. Questions may have been tried out on sample groups, or subjected to statistical analysis, to determine their usefulness.

Written tests are often used in combination with performance tests, ratings of training and experience, and oral interviews. All of these measures combine to form the best-known means of finding the right person for the right job.

II. HOW TO PASS THE WRITTEN TEST

A. NATURE OF THE EXAMINATION

To prepare intelligently for civil service examinations, you should know how they differ from school examinations you have taken. In school you were assigned certain definite pages to read or subjects to cover. The examination questions were quite detailed and usually emphasized memory. Civil service exams, on the other hand, try to discover your present ability to perform the duties of a position, plus your potentiality to learn these duties. In other words, a civil service exam attempts to predict how successful you will be. Questions cover such a broad area that they cannot be as minute and detailed as school exam questions.

In the public service similar kinds of work, or positions, are grouped together in one "class." This process is known as *position-classification*. All the positions in a class are paid according to the salary range for that class. One class title covers all of these positions, and they are all tested by the same examination.

B. FOUR BASIC STEPS

1) Study the announcement

How, then, can you know what subjects to study? Our best answer is: "Learn as much as possible about the class of positions for which you've applied." The exam will test the knowledge, skills and abilities needed to do the work.

Your most valuable source of information about the position you want is the official exam announcement. This announcement lists the training and experience qualifications. Check these standards and apply only if you come reasonably close to meeting them.

The brief description of the position in the examination announcement offers some clues to the subjects which will be tested. Think about the job itself. Review the duties in your mind. Can you perform them, or are there some in which you are rusty? Fill in the blank spots in your preparation.

Many jurisdictions preview the written test in the exam announcement by including a section called "Knowledge and Abilities Required," "Scope of the Examination," or some similar heading. Here you will find out specifically what fields will be tested.

2) Review your own background

Once you learn in general what the position is all about, and what you need to know to do the work, ask yourself which subjects you already know fairly well and which need improvement. You may wonder whether to concentrate on improving your strong areas or on building some background in your fields of weakness. When the announcement has specified "some knowledge" or "considerable knowledge," or has used adjectives like "beginning principles of…" or "advanced … methods," you can get a clue as to the number and difficulty of questions to be asked in any given field. More questions, and hence broader coverage, would be included for those subjects which are more important in the work. Now weigh your strengths and weaknesses against the job requirements and prepare accordingly.

3) Determine the level of the position

Another way to tell how intensively you should prepare is to understand the level of the job for which you are applying. Is it the entering level? In other words, is this the position in which beginners in a field of work are hired? Or is it an intermediate or advanced level? Sometimes this is indicated by such words as "Junior" or "Senior" in the class title. Other jurisdictions use Roman numerals to designate the level – Clerk I, Clerk II, for example. The word "Supervisor" sometimes appears in the title. If the level is not indicated by the title, check the description of duties. Will you be working under very close supervision, or will you have responsibility for independent decisions in this work?

4) Choose appropriate study materials

Now that you know the subjects to be examined and the relative amount of each subject to be covered, you can choose suitable study materials. For beginning level jobs, or even advanced ones, if you have a pronounced weakness in some aspect of your training, read a modern, standard textbook in that field. Be sure it is up to date and has general coverage. Such books are normally available at your library, and the librarian will be glad to help you locate one. For entry-level positions, questions of appropriate difficulty are chosen – neither highly advanced questions, nor those too simple. Such questions require careful thought but not advanced training.

If the position for which you are applying is technical or advanced, you will read more advanced, specialized material. If you are already familiar with the basic principles of your field, elementary textbooks would waste your time. Concentrate on advanced textbooks and technical periodicals. Think through the concepts and review difficult problems in your field.

These are all general sources. You can get more ideas on your own initiative, following these leads. For example, training manuals and publications of the government agency which employs workers in your field can be useful, particularly for technical and professional positions. A letter or visit to the government department involved may result in more specific study suggestions, and certainly will provide you with a more definite idea of the exact nature of the position you are seeking.

III. KINDS OF TESTS

Tests are used for purposes other than measuring knowledge and ability to perform specified duties. For some positions, it is equally important to test ability to make adjustments to new situations or to profit from training. In others, basic mental abilities not dependent on information are essential. Questions which test these things may not appear as pertinent to the duties of the position as those which test for knowledge and information. Yet they are often highly important parts of a fair examination. For very general questions, it is almost impossible to help you direct your study efforts. What we can do is to point out some of the more common of these general abilities needed in public service positions and describe some typical questions.

1) General information

Broad, general information has been found useful for predicting job success in some kinds of work. This is tested in a variety of ways, from vocabulary lists to questions about current events. Basic background in some field of work, such as sociology or economics, may be sampled in a group of questions. Often these are principles which have become familiar to most persons through exposure rather than through formal training. It is difficult to advise you how to study for these questions; being alert to the world around you is our best suggestion.

2) Verbal ability

An example of an ability needed in many positions is verbal or language ability. Verbal ability is, in brief, the ability to use and understand words. Vocabulary and grammar tests are typical measures of this ability. Reading comprehension or paragraph interpretation questions are common in many kinds of civil service tests. You are given a paragraph of written material and asked to find its central meaning.

3) Numerical ability

Number skills can be tested by the familiar arithmetic problem, by checking paired lists of numbers to see which are alike and which are different, or by interpreting charts and graphs. In the latter test, a graph may be printed in the test booklet which you are asked to use as the basis for answering questions.

4) Observation

A popular test for law-enforcement positions is the observation test. A picture is shown to you for several minutes, then taken away. Questions about the picture test your ability to observe both details and larger elements.

5) Following directions

In many positions in the public service, the employee must be able to carry out written instructions dependably and accurately. You may be given a chart with several columns, each column listing a variety of information. The questions require you to carry out directions involving the information given in the chart.

6) Skills and aptitudes

Performance tests effectively measure some manual skills and aptitudes. When the skill is one in which you are trained, such as typing or shorthand, you can practice. These tests are often very much like those given in business school or high school courses. For many of the other skills and aptitudes, however, no short-time preparation can be made. Skills and abilities natural to you or that you have developed throughout your lifetime are being tested.

Many of the general questions just described provide all the data needed to answer the questions and ask you to use your reasoning ability to find the answers. Your best preparation for these tests, as well as for tests of facts and ideas, is to be at your physical and mental best. You, no doubt, have your own methods of getting into an exam-taking mood and keeping "in shape." The next section lists some ideas on this subject.

IV. KINDS OF QUESTIONS

Only rarely is the "essay" question, which you answer in narrative form, used in civil service tests. Civil service tests are usually of the short-answer type. Full instructions for answering these questions will be given to you at the examination. But in case this is your first experience with short-answer questions and separate answer sheets, here is what you need to know:

1) Multiple-choice Questions

Most popular of the short-answer questions is the "multiple choice" or "best answer" question. It can be used, for example, to test for factual knowledge, ability to solve problems or judgment in meeting situations found at work.

A multiple-choice question is normally one of three types—

- It can begin with an incomplete statement followed by several possible endings. You are to find the one ending which *best* completes the statement, although some of the others may not be entirely wrong.
- It can also be a complete statement in the form of a question which is answered by choosing one of the statements listed.
- It can be in the form of a problem – again you select the best answer.

Here is an example of a multiple choice question with a discussion which should give you some clues as to the method for choosing the right answer:

When an employee has a complaint about his assignment, the action which will *best* help him overcome his difficulty is to
  A. discuss his difficulty with his coworkers
  B. take the problem to the head of the organization
  C. take the problem to the person who gave him the assignment
  D. say nothing to anyone about his complaint

In answering this question, you should study each of the choices to find which is best. Consider choice "A" – Certainly an employee may discuss his complaint with fellow employees, but no change or improvement can result, and the complaint remains unresolved. Choice "B" is a poor choice since the head of the organization probably does not know what assignment you have been given, and taking your problem to him is known as "going over the head" of the supervisor. The supervisor, or person who made the assignment, is the person who can clarify it or correct any injustice. Choice "C" is, therefore, correct. To say nothing, as in choice "D," is unwise. Supervisors have and interest in knowing the problems employees are facing, and the employee is seeking a solution to his problem.

2) True/False Questions

The "true/false" or "right/wrong" form of question is sometimes used. Here a complete statement is given. Your job is to decide whether the statement is right or wrong.

SAMPLE: A person-to-person long-distance telephone call costs less than a station-to-station call to the same city.

This statement is wrong, or false, since person-to-person calls are more expensive.

This is not a complete list of all possible question forms, although most of the others are variations of these common types. You will always get complete directions for answering questions. Be sure you understand *how* to mark your answers – ask questions until you do.

V. RECORDING YOUR ANSWERS

For an examination with very few applicants, you may be told to record your answers in the test booklet itself. Separate answer sheets are much more common. If this separate answer sheet is to be scored by machine – and this is often the case – it is highly important that you mark your answers correctly in order to get credit.

An electric scoring machine is often used in civil service offices because of the speed with which papers can be scored. Machine-scored answer sheets must be marked with a pencil, which will be given to you. This pencil has a high graphite content which responds to the electric scoring machine. As a matter of fact, stray dots may register as answers, so do not let your pencil rest on the answer sheet while you are pondering the correct answer. Also, if your pencil lead breaks or is otherwise defective, ask for another.

Since the answer sheet will be dropped in a slot in the scoring machine, be careful not to bend the corners or get the paper crumpled.

The answer sheet normally has five vertical columns of numbers, with 30 numbers to a column. These numbers correspond to the question numbers in your test booklet. After each number, going across the page are four or five pairs of dotted lines. These short dotted lines have small letters or numbers above them. The first two pairs may also have a "T" or "F" above the letters. This indicates that the first two pairs only are to be used if the questions are of the true-false type. If the questions are multiple choice, disregard the "T" and "F" and pay attention only to the small letters or numbers.

Answer your questions in the manner of the sample that follows:

32. The largest city in the United States is
    A. Washington, D.C.
    B. New York City
    C. Chicago
    D. Detroit
    E. San Francisco

1) Choose the answer you think is best. (New York City is the largest, so "B" is correct.)
2) Find the row of dotted lines numbered the same as the question you are answering. (Find row number 32)
3) Find the pair of dotted lines corresponding to the answer. (Find the pair of lines under the mark "B.")
4) Make a solid black mark between the dotted lines.

VI. BEFORE THE TEST

Common sense will help you find procedures to follow to get ready for an examination. Too many of us, however, overlook these sensible measures. Indeed, nervousness and fatigue have been found to be the most serious reasons why applicants fail to do their best on civil service tests. Here is a list of reminders:

- Begin your preparation early – Don't wait until the last minute to go scurrying around for books and materials or to find out what the position is all about.
- Prepare continuously – An hour a night for a week is better than an all-night cram session. This has been definitely established. What is more, a night a

week for a month will return better dividends than crowding your study into a shorter period of time.

- Locate the place of the exam – You have been sent a notice telling you when and where to report for the examination. If the location is in a different town or otherwise unfamiliar to you, it would be well to inquire the best route and learn something about the building.
- Relax the night before the test – Allow your mind to rest. Do not study at all that night. Plan some mild recreation or diversion; then go to bed early and get a good night's sleep.
- Get up early enough to make a leisurely trip to the place for the test – This way unforeseen events, traffic snarls, unfamiliar buildings, etc. will not upset you.
- Dress comfortably – A written test is not a fashion show. You will be known by number and not by name, so wear something comfortable.
- Leave excess paraphernalia at home – Shopping bags and odd bundles will get in your way. You need bring only the items mentioned in the official notice you received; usually everything you need is provided. Do not bring reference books to the exam. They will only confuse those last minutes and be taken away from you when in the test room.
- Arrive somewhat ahead of time – If because of transportation schedules you must get there very early, bring a newspaper or magazine to take your mind off yourself while waiting.
- Locate the examination room – When you have found the proper room, you will be directed to the seat or part of the room where you will sit. Sometimes you are given a sheet of instructions to read while you are waiting. Do not fill out any forms until you are told to do so; just read them and be prepared.
- Relax and prepare to listen to the instructions
- If you have any physical problem that may keep you from doing your best, be sure to tell the test administrator. If you are sick or in poor health, you really cannot do your best on the exam. You can come back and take the test some other time.

VII. AT THE TEST

The day of the test is here and you have the test booklet in your hand. The temptation to get going is very strong. Caution! There is more to success than knowing the right answers. You must know how to identify your papers and understand variations in the type of short-answer question used in this particular examination. Follow these suggestions for maximum results from your efforts:

1) Cooperate with the monitor

The test administrator has a duty to create a situation in which you can be as much at ease as possible. He will give instructions, tell you when to begin, check to see that you are marking your answer sheet correctly, and so on. He is not there to guard you, although he will see that your competitors do not take unfair advantage. He wants to help you do your best.

2) Listen to all instructions

Don't jump the gun! Wait until you understand all directions. In most civil service tests you get more time than you need to answer the questions. So don't be in a hurry.

Read each word of instructions until you clearly understand the meaning. Study the examples, listen to all announcements and follow directions. Ask questions if you do not understand what to do.

3) Identify your papers

Civil service exams are usually identified by number only. You will be assigned a number; you must not put your name on your test papers. Be sure to copy your number correctly. Since more than one exam may be given, copy your exact examination title.

4) Plan your time

Unless you are told that a test is a "speed" or "rate of work" test, speed itself is usually not important. Time enough to answer all the questions will be provided, but this does not mean that you have all day. An overall time limit has been set. Divide the total time (in minutes) by the number of questions to determine the approximate time you have for each question.

5) Do not linger over difficult questions

If you come across a difficult question, mark it with a paper clip (useful to have along) and come back to it when you have been through the booklet. One caution if you do this – be sure to skip a number on your answer sheet as well. Check often to be sure that you have not lost your place and that you are marking in the row numbered the same as the question you are answering.

6) Read the questions

Be sure you know what the question asks! Many capable people are unsuccessful because they failed to *read* the questions correctly.

7) Answer all questions

Unless you have been instructed that a penalty will be deducted for incorrect answers, it is better to guess than to omit a question.

8) Speed tests

It is often better NOT to guess on speed tests. It has been found that on timed tests people are tempted to spend the last few seconds before time is called in marking answers at random – without even reading them – in the hope of picking up a few extra points. To discourage this practice, the instructions may warn you that your score will be "corrected" for guessing. That is, a penalty will be applied. The incorrect answers will be deducted from the correct ones, or some other penalty formula will be used.

9) Review your answers

If you finish before time is called, go back to the questions you guessed or omitted to give them further thought. Review other answers if you have time.

10) Return your test materials

If you are ready to leave before others have finished or time is called, take ALL your materials to the monitor and leave quietly. Never take any test material with you. The monitor can discover whose papers are not complete, and taking a test booklet may be grounds for disqualification.

VIII. EXAMINATION TECHNIQUES

1) Read the general instructions carefully. These are usually printed on the first page of the exam booklet. As a rule, these instructions refer to the timing of the examination; the fact that you should not start work until the signal and must stop work at a signal, etc. If there are any *special* instructions, such as a choice of questions to be answered, make sure that you note this instruction carefully.

2) When you are ready to start work on the examination, that is as soon as the signal has been given, read the instructions to each question booklet, underline any key words or phrases, such as *least, best, outline, describe* and the like. In this way you will tend to answer as requested rather than discover on reviewing your paper that you *listed without describing*, that you selected the *worst* choice rather than the *best* choice, etc.

3) If the examination is of the objective or multiple-choice type – that is, each question will also give a series of possible answers: A, B, C or D, and you are called upon to select the best answer and write the letter next to that answer on your answer paper – it is advisable to start answering each question in turn. There may be anywhere from 50 to 100 such questions in the three or four hours allotted and you can see how much time would be taken if you read through all the questions before beginning to answer any. Furthermore, if you come across a question or group of questions which you know would be difficult to answer, it would undoubtedly affect your handling of all the other questions.

4) If the examination is of the essay type and contains but a few questions, it is a moot point as to whether you should read all the questions before starting to answer any one. Of course, if you are given a choice – say five out of seven and the like – then it is essential to read all the questions so you can eliminate the two that are most difficult. If, however, you are asked to answer all the questions, there may be danger in trying to answer the easiest one first because you may find that you will spend too much time on it. The best technique is to answer the first question, then proceed to the second, etc.

5) Time your answers. Before the exam begins, write down the time it started, then add the time allowed for the examination and write down the time it must be completed, then divide the time available somewhat as follows:
   - If 3-1/2 hours are allowed, that would be 210 minutes. If you have 80 objective-type questions, that would be an average of 2-1/2 minutes per question. Allow yourself no more than 2 minutes per question, or a total of 160 minutes, which will permit about 50 minutes to review.
   - If for the time allotment of 210 minutes there are 7 essay questions to answer, that would average about 30 minutes a question. Give yourself only 25 minutes per question so that you have about 35 minutes to review.

6) The most important instruction is to *read each question* and make sure you know what is wanted. The second most important instruction is to *time yourself properly* so that you answer every question. The third most

important instruction is to *answer every question*. Guess if you have to but include something for each question. Remember that you will receive no credit for a blank and will probably receive some credit if you write something in answer to an essay question. If you guess a letter – say "B" for a multiple-choice question – you may have guessed right. If you leave a blank as an answer to a multiple-choice question, the examiners may respect your feelings but it will not add a point to your score. Some exams may penalize you for wrong answers, so in such cases *only*, you may not want to guess unless you have some basis for your answer.

7) Suggestions
   a. Objective-type questions
     1. Examine the question booklet for proper sequence of pages and questions
     2. Read all instructions carefully
     3. Skip any question which seems too difficult; return to it after all other questions have been answered
     4. Apportion your time properly; do not spend too much time on any single question or group of questions
     5. Note and underline key words – *all, most, fewest, least, best, worst, same, opposite,* etc.
     6. Pay particular attention to negatives
     7. Note unusual option, e.g., unduly long, short, complex, different or similar in content to the body of the question
     8. Observe the use of "hedging" words – *probably, may, most likely,* etc.
     9. Make sure that your answer is put next to the same number as the question
     10. Do not second-guess unless you have good reason to believe the second answer is definitely more correct
     11. Cross out original answer if you decide another answer is more accurate; do not erase until you are ready to hand your paper in
     12. Answer all questions; guess unless instructed otherwise
     13. Leave time for review

   b. Essay questions
     1. Read each question carefully
     2. Determine exactly what is wanted. Underline key words or phrases.
     3. Decide on outline or paragraph answer
     4. Include many different points and elements unless asked to develop any one or two points or elements
     5. Show impartiality by giving pros and cons unless directed to select one side only
     6. Make and write down any assumptions you find necessary to answer the questions
     7. Watch your English, grammar, punctuation and choice of words
     8. Time your answers; don't crowd material

8) Answering the essay question

Most essay questions can be answered by framing the specific response around several key words or ideas. Here are a few such key words or ideas:

M's: manpower, materials, methods, money, management
P's: purpose, program, policy, plan, procedure, practice, problems, pitfalls, personnel, public relations

a. Six basic steps in handling problems:
1. Preliminary plan and background development
2. Collect information, data and facts
3. Analyze and interpret information, data and facts
4. Analyze and develop solutions as well as make recommendations
5. Prepare report and sell recommendations
6. Install recommendations and follow up effectiveness

b. Pitfalls to avoid
1. *Taking things for granted* – A statement of the situation does not necessarily imply that each of the elements is necessarily true; for example, a complaint may be invalid and biased so that all that can be taken for granted is that a complaint has been registered
2. *Considering only one side of a situation* – Wherever possible, indicate several alternatives and then point out the reasons you selected the best one
3. *Failing to indicate follow up* – Whenever your answer indicates action on your part, make certain that you will take proper follow-up action to see how successful your recommendations, procedures or actions turn out to be
4. *Taking too long in answering any single question* – Remember to time your answers properly

IX. AFTER THE TEST

Scoring procedures differ in detail among civil service jurisdictions although the general principles are the same. Whether the papers are hand-scored or graded by machine we have described, they are nearly always graded by number. That is, the person who marks the paper knows only the number – never the name – of the applicant. Not until all the papers have been graded will they be matched with names. If other tests, such as training and experience or oral interview ratings have been given, scores will be combined. Different parts of the examination usually have different weights. For example, the written test might count 60 percent of the final grade, and a rating of training and experience 40 percent. In many jurisdictions, veterans will have a certain number of points added to their grades.

After the final grade has been determined, the names are placed in grade order and an eligible list is established. There are various methods for resolving ties between those who get the same final grade – probably the most common is to place first the name of the person whose application was received first. Job offers are made from the eligible list in the order the names appear on it. You will be notified of your grade and your rank as soon as all these computations have been made. This will be done as rapidly as possible.

People who are found to meet the requirements in the announcement are called "eligibles." Their names are put on a list of eligible candidates. An eligible's chances of getting a job depend on how high he stands on this list and how fast agencies are filling jobs from the list.

When a job is to be filled from a list of eligibles, the agency asks for the names of people on the list of eligibles for that job. When the civil service commission receives this request, it sends to the agency the names of the three people highest on this list. Or, if the job to be filled has specialized requirements, the office sends the agency the names of the top three persons who meet these requirements from the general list.

The appointing officer makes a choice from among the three people whose names were sent to him. If the selected person accepts the appointment, the names of the others are put back on the list to be considered for future openings.

That is the rule in hiring from all kinds of eligible lists, whether they are for typist, carpenter, chemist, or something else. For every vacancy, the appointing officer has his choice of any one of the top three eligibles on the list. This explains why the person whose name is on top of the list sometimes does not get an appointment when some of the persons lower on the list do. If the appointing officer chooses the second or third eligible, the No. 1 eligible does not get a job at once, but stays on the list until he is appointed or the list is terminated.

X. HOW TO PASS THE INTERVIEW TEST

The examination for which you applied requires an oral interview test. You have already taken the written test and you are now being called for the interview test – the final part of the formal examination.

You may think that it is not possible to prepare for an interview test and that there are no procedures to follow during an interview. Our purpose is to point out some things you can do in advance that will help you and some good rules to follow and pitfalls to avoid while you are being interviewed.

What is an interview supposed to test?

The written examination is designed to test the technical knowledge and competence of the candidate; the oral is designed to evaluate intangible qualities, not readily measured otherwise, and to establish a list showing the relative fitness of each candidate – as measured against his competitors – for the position sought. Scoring is not on the basis of "right" and "wrong," but on a sliding scale of values ranging from "not passable" to "outstanding." As a matter of fact, it is possible to achieve a relatively low score without a single "incorrect" answer because of evident weakness in the qualities being measured.

Occasionally, an examination may consist entirely of an oral test – either an individual or a group oral. In such cases, information is sought concerning the technical knowledges and abilities of the candidate, since there has been no written examination for this purpose. More commonly, however, an oral test is used to supplement a written examination.

Who conducts interviews?

The composition of oral boards varies among different jurisdictions. In nearly all, a representative of the personnel department serves as chairman. One of the members of the board may be a representative of the department in which the candidate would work. In some cases, "outside experts" are used, and, frequently, a businessman or some other representative of the general public is asked to serve. Labor and management or other special groups may be represented. The aim is to secure the services of experts in the appropriate field.

However the board is composed, it is a good idea (and not at all improper or unethical) to ascertain in advance of the interview who the members are and what groups they represent. When you are introduced to them, you will have some idea of their backgrounds and interests, and at least you will not stutter and stammer over their names.

What should be done before the interview?

While knowledge about the board members is useful and takes some of the surprise element out of the interview, there is other preparation which is more substantive. It *is* possible to prepare for an oral interview – in several ways:

1) Keep a copy of your application and review it carefully before the interview

This may be the only document before the oral board, and the starting point of the interview. Know what education and experience you have listed there, and the sequence and dates of all of it. Sometimes the board will ask you to review the highlights of your experience for them; you should not have to hem and haw doing it.

2) Study the class specification and the examination announcement

Usually, the oral board has one or both of these to guide them. The qualities, characteristics or knowledges required by the position sought are stated in these documents. They offer valuable clues as to the nature of the oral interview. For example, if the job involves supervisory responsibilities, the announcement will usually indicate that knowledge of modern supervisory methods and the qualifications of the candidate as a supervisor will be tested. If so, you can expect such questions, frequently in the form of a hypothetical situation which you are expected to solve. NEVER go into an oral without knowledge of the duties and responsibilities of the job you seek.

3) Think through each qualification required

Try to visualize the kind of questions you would ask if you were a board member. How well could you answer them? Try especially to appraise your own knowledge and background in each area, *measured against the job sought*, and identify any areas in which you are weak. Be critical and realistic – do not flatter yourself.

4) Do some general reading in areas in which you feel you may be weak

For example, if the job involves supervision and your past experience has NOT, some general reading in supervisory methods and practices, particularly in the field of human relations, might be useful. Do NOT study agency procedures or detailed manuals. The oral board will be testing your understanding and capacity, not your memory.

5) Get a good night's sleep and watch your general health and mental attitude

You will want a clear head at the interview. Take care of a cold or any other minor ailment, and of course, no hangovers.

What should be done on the day of the interview?

Now comes the day of the interview itself. Give yourself plenty of time to get there. Plan to arrive somewhat ahead of the scheduled time, particularly if your appointment is in the fore part of the day. If a previous candidate fails to appear, the board might be ready for you a bit early. By early afternoon an oral board is almost invariably behind schedule if there are many candidates, and you may have to wait.

Take along a book or magazine to read, or your application to review, but leave any extraneous material in the waiting room when you go in for your interview. In any event, relax and compose yourself.

The matter of dress is important. The board is forming impressions about you – from your experience, your manners, your attitude, and your appearance. Give your personal appearance careful attention. Dress your best, but not your flashiest. Choose conservative, appropriate clothing, and be sure it is immaculate. This is a business interview, and your appearance should indicate that you regard it as such. Besides, being well groomed and properly dressed will help boost your confidence.

Sooner or later, someone will call your name and escort you into the interview room. *This is it.* From here on you are on your own. It is too late for any more preparation. But remember, you asked for this opportunity to prove your fitness, and you are here because your request was granted.

What happens when you go in?

The usual sequence of events will be as follows: The clerk (who is often the board stenographer) will introduce you to the chairman of the oral board, who will introduce you to the other members of the board. Acknowledge the introductions before you sit down. Do not be surprised if you find a microphone facing you or a stenotypist sitting by. Oral interviews are usually recorded in the event of an appeal or other review.

Usually the chairman of the board will open the interview by reviewing the highlights of your education and work experience from your application – primarily for the benefit of the other members of the board, as well as to get the material into the record. Do not interrupt or comment unless there is an error or significant misinterpretation; if that is the case, do not hesitate. But do not quibble about insignificant matters. Also, he will usually ask you some question about your education, experience or your present job – partly to get you to start talking and to establish the interviewing "rapport." He may start the actual questioning, or turn it over to one of the other members. Frequently, each member undertakes the questioning on a particular area, one in which he is perhaps most competent, so you can expect each member to participate in the examination. Because time is limited, you may also expect some rather abrupt switches in the direction the questioning takes, so do not be upset by it. Normally, a board member will not pursue a single line of questioning unless he discovers a particular strength or weakness.

After each member has participated, the chairman will usually ask whether any member has any further questions, then will ask you if you have anything you wish to add. Unless you are expecting this question, it may floor you. Worse, it may start you off on an extended, extemporaneous speech. The board is not usually seeking more information. The question is principally to offer you a last opportunity to present further qualifications or to indicate that you have nothing to add. So, if you feel that a significant qualification or characteristic has been overlooked, it is proper to point it out in a sentence or so. Do not compliment the board on the thoroughness of their examination – they have been sketchy, and you know it. If you wish, merely say, "No thank you, I have nothing further to add." This is a point where you can "talk yourself out" of a good impression or fail to present an important bit of information. Remember, *you close the interview yourself.*

The chairman will then say, "That is all, Mr. _____, thank you." Do not be startled; the interview is over, and quicker than you think. Thank him, gather your belongings and take your leave. Save your sigh of relief for the other side of the door.

How to put your best foot forward

Throughout this entire process, you may feel that the board individually and collectively is trying to pierce your defenses, seek out your hidden weaknesses and embarrass and confuse you. Actually, this is not true. They are obliged to make an appraisal of your qualifications for the job you are seeking, and they want to see you in your best light. Remember, they must interview all candidates and a non-cooperative candidate may become a failure in spite of their best efforts to bring out his qualifications. Here are 15 suggestions that will help you:

1) Be natural – Keep your attitude confident, not cocky

If you are not confident that you can do the job, do not expect the board to be. Do not apologize for your weaknesses, try to bring out your strong points. The board is interested in a positive, not negative, presentation. Cockiness will antagonize any board member and make him wonder if you are covering up a weakness by a false show of strength.

2) Get comfortable, but don't lounge or sprawl

Sit erectly but not stiffly. A careless posture may lead the board to conclude that you are careless in other things, or at least that you are not impressed by the importance of the occasion. Either conclusion is natural, even if incorrect. Do not fuss with your clothing, a pencil or an ashtray. Your hands may occasionally be useful to emphasize a point, do not let them become a point of distraction.

3) Do not wisecrack or make small talk

This is a serious situation, and your attitude should show that you consider it as such. Further, the time of the board is limited – they do not want to waste it, and neither should you.

4) Do not exaggerate your experience or abilities

In the first place, from information in the application or other interviews and sources, the board may know more about you than you think. Secondly, you probably will not get away with it. An experienced board is rather adept at spotting such a situation, so do not take the chance.

5) If you know a board member, do not make a point of it, yet do not hide it

Certainly you are not fooling him, and probably not the other members of the board. Do not try to take advantage of your acquaintanceship – it will probably do you little good.

6) Do not dominate the interview

Let the board do that. They will give you the clues – do not assume that you have to do all the talking. Realize that the board has a number of questions to ask you, and do not try to take up all the interview time by showing off your extensive knowledge of the answer to the first one.

7) Be attentive

You only have 20 minutes or so, and you should keep your attention at its sharpest throughout. When a member is addressing a problem or question to you, give him your undivided attention. Address your reply principally to him, but do not exclude the other board members.

8) Do not interrupt

A board member may be stating a problem for you to analyze. He will ask you a question when the time comes. Let him state the problem, and wait for the question.

9) Make sure you understand the question

Do not try to answer until you are sure what the question is. If it is not clear, restate it in your own words or ask the board member to clarify it for you. However, do not haggle about minor elements.

10) Reply promptly but not hastily

A common entry on oral board rating sheets is "candidate responded readily," or "candidate hesitated in replies." Respond as promptly and quickly as you can, but do not jump to a hasty, ill-considered answer.

11) Do not be peremptory in your answers

A brief answer is proper – but do not fire your answer back. That is a losing game from your point of view. The board member can probably ask questions much faster than you can answer them.

12) Do not try to create the answer you think the board member wants

He is interested in what kind of mind you have and how it works – not in playing games. Furthermore, he can usually spot this practice and will actually grade you down on it.

13) Do not switch sides in your reply merely to agree with a board member

Frequently, a member will take a contrary position merely to draw you out and to see if you are willing and able to defend your point of view. Do not start a debate, yet do not surrender a good position. If a position is worth taking, it is worth defending.

14) Do not be afraid to admit an error in judgment if you are shown to be wrong

The board knows that you are forced to reply without any opportunity for careful consideration. Your answer may be demonstrably wrong. If so, admit it and get on with the interview.

15) Do not dwell at length on your present job

The opening question may relate to your present assignment. Answer the question but do not go into an extended discussion. You are being examined for a *new* job, not your present one. As a matter of fact, try to phrase ALL your answers in terms of the job for which you are being examined.

Basis of Rating

Probably you will forget most of these "do's" and "don'ts" when you walk into the oral interview room. Even remembering them all will not ensure you a passing grade. Perhaps you did not have the qualifications in the first place. But remembering them will help you to put your best foot forward, without treading on the toes of the board members.

Rumor and popular opinion to the contrary notwithstanding, an oral board wants you to make the best appearance possible. They know you are under pressure – but they also want to see how you respond to it as a guide to what your reaction would be under the pressures of the job you seek. They will be influenced by the degree of poise you display, the personal traits you show and the manner in which you respond.

EXAMINATION SECTION

ELECTRICITY
EXAMINATION SECTION
TEST 1

DIRECTIONS: Each question or incomplete statement is followed by
several suggested answers or completions. Select the
one that BEST answers the question or completes the
statement. *PRINT THE LETTER OF THE CORRECT ANSWER IN
THE SPACE AT THE RIGHT.*

1. The electrical code requires that the controller for an   1._____
    A.C. motor shall be capable of interrupting
    A. twice the full load current of the motor
    B. three times the full load current of the motor
    C. five times the full load current of the motor
    D. the stalled rotor current

2. The MINIMUM number of overload devices required for a   2._____
    3Ø A.C. motor connected to a 120/208 volt system is
    A. 1   B. 2   C. 3   D. 4

3. A feeder tap shall be considered as properly protected   3._____
    when the smaller conductors terminate in a single properly
    sized set of fuses or a circuit breaker, provided the
    A. tap is not over 25 feet long
    B. tap is not over 15 feet long
    C. current carrying capacity of the tap is at least 1/3
       the rating of the fuse or circuit breaker protecting
       the main
    D. tap is not over 25 feet long and its current carrying
       capacity is at least 1/3 the rating of the fuse
       protecting the main

4. Branch circuit conductors supplying a motor shall have a   4._____
    current carrying capacity, in percentage of the full load
    current rating of the motor, of NOT less than
    A. 100%   B. 125%   C. 150%   D. 200%

5. The motor disconnecting means shall be located   5._____
    A. within 10 feet of the motor
    B. within sight of the controller
    C. within 15 feet of the motor
    D. where convenient

6. The motor disconnecting means shall have a continuous   6._____
    duty rating, in percentage of the name plate current
    rating of the motor, of AT LEAST
    A. 100%   B. 115%   C. 150%   D. 125%

7. An externally operable switch may be used as a starter for   7.___
   a motor not over 2 HP and not over 300 volts provided it
   has a rating of AT LEAST _____ of the _____ current of
   the motor.
   A. 200%; stalled rotor   B. 200%; full load
   C. 115%; full load   D. 150%; stalled rotor

8. A single disconnecting means may serve a group of motors   8.___
   provided
   A. all motors are 1/2 HP or less
   B. all motors are within a short distance from each other
   C. all motors are located within a single room and with-
      in sight of the disconnecting means
   D. one-half of the motors are located within a single
      room and within sight of the disconnecting means

9. A single-throw knife switch should be mounted so that   9.___
   A. gravity tends to close it
   B. it is in a vertical position
   C. it is accessible only to qualified persons
   D. gravity tends to open it

10. For oil burner motors, the disconnecting means shall be   10.___
    placed
    A. on the oil burner
    B. at the entrance to the basement
    C. inside the oil burner room
    D. not necessary

11. The MAIN reason for grounding conduit is to prevent it   11.___
    from becoming
    A. corroded by electrolysis
    B. magnetized
    C. accidentally energized at a higher potential than
       ground
    D. a source of radio interference

12. Large wires or cables are to pulled through conduit where   12.___
    there are a number of bends.
    This operation may be made easier by applying to the sur-
    face of these wires or cables a limited quantity of
    A. soapstone or talc   B. oil
    C. grease   D. rosin

13. Assume that a poly-phase synchronous converter having a   13.___
    field splitting or sectionalizing switch and a series
    field diverter is to be started from the A.C. side.
    When starting from the A.C. side, the sectionalizing
    switch should be _____ and the diverter should be _____.
    A. closed; closed   B. closed; opened
    C. opened; closed   D. opened; opened

14. In the electrical trade, the tool USUALLY used for bending 14.___
    small size pipe is a
    A. pipe hickey   B. grooved sheave bender
    C. roller bender   D. pipe wrench

15. For supplying both motor and lighting load, the type of A.C. distribution system commonly used is _____ wire.
    A. 2Ø – 4   B. 1Ø – 3   C. 3Ø – 3   D. 3Ø – 4

    15.___

16. A set of conductors originating at a distribution center other than the main distribution center, and supplying one or more branch circuit distribution centers, is known as
    A. subservice   B. main
    C. subfeeder   D. feeder

    16.___

17. A lighting distribution panel board is to be fed from a 1Ø 3-wire grounded neutral A.C. feeder.
    The MAXIMUM number of 2-wire branch circuits that this panel board may supply is
    A. 20   B. 36
    C. 42   D. any number

    17.___

18. The type of socket that must be used for a 500 watt incandescent lamp is _____ base.
    A. screw shell medium   B. mogul
    C. intermediate   D. candelabra

    18.___

19. The number of quarter bends between conduit fitting or boxes including those at the fitting or box shall NOT exceed
    A. 2   B. 4   C. 6   D. 8

    19.___

20. A grounding conductor for portable or fixed equipment shall be
    A. white   B. grey   C. green   D. black

    20.___

21. One foot of a certain size of nichrome wire has a resistance of 2 ohms.
    To make a heating element for a 600 watt, 120 volt toaster, the number of feet required is
    A. 5   B. 10   C. 12   D. 24

    21.___

22. Which of the following wires has the LARGEST current carrying capacity?
    A. Asbestos   B. Rubber
    C. Waxed cotton   D. Thermoplastic

    22.___

23. According to the electrical code, the sum of the continuous rating of the load consuming apparatus connected to the system or part of the system is defined as the _____ load of the system.
    A. computed   B. connected   C. calculated   D. rated

    23.___

24. When fuses are used as motor protection, they shall be placed in
    A. all ungrounded conductors
    B. all conductors
    C. all but one ungrounded conductor
    D. half of the ungrounded conductors

    24.___

25. Except for circuits of a system having a grounded neutral having no conductor at more than 150 volts to ground, plug fuses shall not be used in circuits where the voltage EXCEEDS ____ volts.

25.___

     A. 110   B. 125   C. 150   D. 250

TEST 2

1. Collector wires for a crane are supported at 25 foot intervals.
   The MINIMUM wire size that may be used is #

1.___

     A. 2   B. 4   C. 6   D. 8

2. It is necessary to space insulating supports for main collector wires of a crane forty feet apart.
   The wires run on the same horizontal plane must be separated ____ inches.

2.___

     A. 3   B. 6   C. 8   D. 12

3. A reverse phase relay is a device which is PRIMARILY used

3.___

     A. to reverse rotation of 3-phase induction motors
     B. to prevent accidental reversal of a polyphase motor
     C. to reverse the current in case one phase is reversed
     D. as an overload relay for 3-phase motors

4. A 3∅ motor used on a crane or a hoist

4.___

     A. will not start if one phase is not live
     B. will not start with all resistance inserted
     C. will not start if brake solonoid is energized
     D. may use a common return wire

5. A branch circuit feed for a crane motor that runs through a room where the temperature exceeds 167°F (75°C) shall be type

5.___

     A. R   B. SB
     C. AF   D. fire retarded

6. A common return is used to feed 2 - 3∅ crane motors.
It shall be

6.___

     A. installed in rigid conduit
     B. type AVA
     C. not permitted
     D. individually bushed

7. Surgical operating rooms GENERALLY shall be considered ____ hazardous location(s).

7.___

     A. Class I   B. Class II   C. Class III   D. not a

8. Electrical installations in garages, unless located at least four feet above the floor, shall be governed by the requirements for
   A. Class I   B. Class II
   C. Class III   D. General wiring

8.___

9. Portable extension light cords used in a garage shall NOT exceed _____ feet.
   A. 8   B. 15   C. 20   D. 40

9.___

10. An underground service to a private garage shall be
    A. lead-covered conductors in rigid conduit or other approved types buried 18" or more
    B. lead-covered conductors in rigid conduit buried 12"
    C. lead-covered conductors in E.M.T. buried 18"
    D. type R conductors in rigid conduit buried 18"

10.___

11. High tension conductors for a skeleton sign shall
    A. be insulated for 10,000 volts
    B. be insulated for 15,000 volts
    C. be insulated for 30,000 volts
    D. not be used

11.___

12. Emergency lighting in a theatre shall be controlled
    A. from the stage lighting control
    B. from the lobby
    C. by double pole switches
    D. from the operators booth

12.___

13. The MINIMUM size system grounding conductor shall be NOT less than #
    A. 16   B. 8   C. 4   D. 1/0

13.___

14. If you had a choice of connecting to one of the following grounding electrodes, you would use
    A. buried plates
    B. driven rod
    C. gas piping system
    D. continuous metallic underground active water piping system

14.___

15. Grounding electrodes other than water piping systems shall have a resistance to ground NOT exceeding _____ ohms.
    A. 0   B. 5   C. 25   D. infinity

15.___

16. A grounding conductor for portable or fixed equipment shall be
    A. white   B. grey   C. green   D. black

16.___

17. The MAXIMUM number of outlets allowed on a 20 ampere branch lighting circuit is
    A. 2   B. 8   C. 10   D. 20

17.___

18. The MAXIMUM number of mogul sockets that may be used on a 115 volt heavy duty lampholder branch circuit is
    A. 2   B. 8   C. 10   D. 20

18.___

19. The voltage drop in a 120 volt lighting circuit should be kept to a minimum and may NOT exceed ____ volts.   19. ___
    A. 120   B. 5.2   C. 3   D. 2.5

20. A wire 100 feet long is divided into two parts so that the ratio of their lengths is 4/1.   20. ___
    The length of the longer piece is ____ feet.
    A. 10   B. 20   C. 40   D. 80

21. An effect caused by dissimilar metals is known as   21. ___
    A. thermoelectric   B. thermopile
    C. thermostatic   D. thermionic

22. With the weight of water used as a base, the ratio of weight to other liquids is known as   22. ___
    A. density   B. specific gravity
    C. viscosity   D. buoyancy

23. A utility company would supply a lighting and power load with ____ wire service.   23. ___
    A. 1∅-3   B. 2∅-3   C. 3∅-3   D. 3∅-4

24. A ballast in a fluorescent fixture is used to   24. ___
    A. reduce A.C. hum   B. limit the current
    C. lower capacitor voltage   D. eliminate cycle flicker

25. A fluorescent lamp being basically an A.C. lamp   25. ___
    A. cannot be used D.C.
    B. may be made adaptable for D.C. by connecting a fixed resistor of the proper value in series with the line and auxiliary
    C. may be used for D.C. providing the operating voltage is the same as that required for A.C.
    D. can be used on D.C. only when available voltage is higher than that required for operation on A.C.

TEST 3

1. The MAXIMUM voltage to ground for elevator control push-buttons is ____ volts.   1. ___
    A. 120   B. 208   C. 300   D. 600

2. The MINIMUM size equipment grounding conductor for high tension vertical distribution transformer cases is #   2. ___
    A. 10   B. 8   C. 000   D. 0000

3. Vertical conduits for high tension steel armored cable shall be supported by building construction at intervals NOT exceeding ____ feet and encased in ____ of concrete.   3. ___
    A. 25; 2"   B. 35; 2   C. 35; 3   D. 25; 3

4. The MINIMUM distance that shall be maintained between bare metal parts having a potential difference of 125 volts on panelboards is
    A. 3/4"   B. 1"   C. 1¼"   D. 1½"

4.___

5. The frequency of the current at a load, as compared to that of the generator,
    A. depends on the load   B. is lower
    C. is higher   D. is the same

5.___

6. The resistance to the flow of magnetic flux is known as
    A. permeance   B. reluctance
    C. resistance   D. reactance

6.___

7. A conductor cutting magnetic lines of force at the rate of 10^8 lines per second will generate 1
    A. ohm   B. ampere   C. watt   D. volt

7.___

8. An inverse time delay relay will operate _____ current.
    A. slower, the greater the
    B. faster, the greater the
    C. faster, the smaller the
    D. at the same speed regardless of the amount of

8.___

9. A 120 volt system feeds an arc lamp that is to operate at 15 amps, at 62 volts.
   What resistance must be inserted in the line for PROPER operation?
   _____ ohms.
    A. .26   B. 3.86   C. 4.13   D. 8

9.___

10. If you reversed the line leads to a D.C. compound motor, it would
    A. stop
    B. reverse
    C. run in the same direction
    D. slow down

10.___

11. A D.C. generator has an EMF of 115 volts and an internal resistance of .07 ohms.
    What is the voltage at the load when it is delivering 50 amperes?
    A. 111.5   B. 115   C. 118.5   D. 120

11.___

12. The sockets allowed for a 500 watt incandescent lamp is
    A. candelabra   B. intermediate
    C. medium   D. mogul

12.___

13. A single circuit may be used to feed several small motors, providing the largest motor does NOT exceed _____ amps.
    A. 6   B. 10   C. 15   D. 20

13.___

14. A compensator is a device used with induction motors to   14.___
    A. compensate for electrical losses of the motor
    B. compensate for volt drop in the motor
    C. increase the starting torque of the motor
    D. decrease the line voltage at starting

15. A 2 HP 3-phase 220 volt squirrel cage motor would USUALLY   15.___
    be started by means of a(n)
    A. compensator   B. 3 or 4 point starting box
    C. reduced voltage starter D. across the line starter

16. The type of starting and speed control equipment that   16.___
    would be used for a 50 HP wound rotor induction motor is
    A. with resistors connected in rotor circuit
    B. a 3 point starting box
    C. an autotransformer (compensator)
    D. an automatic primary resistor type of starter

17. In order to reverse rotation of a 3-phase squirrel cage   17.___
    induction motor, you would reverse
    A. any two line leads   B. all line leads
    C. the brush leads   D. starting winding leads

18. Reversing direction of rotation of a 3Ø wound rotor motor   18.___
    could be done by reversing _____ leads.
    A. all slip-ring   B. all line
    C. two slip-ring   D. two line

19. To change direction of rotation of a 4-wire 2-phase motor,   19.___
    A. interchange the leads of one phase
    B. interchange the leads of both phases
    C. reverse the leads from the slip rings
    D. do nothing, it cannot be readily reversed

20. In selecting a reversing type motor starter, for maximum   20.___
    protection, you would choose one that is
    A. separately controlled
    B. mechanically and electrically interlocked
    C. electrically interlocked
    D. mechanically interlocked

21. A 3Ø wound rotor motor running at full speed suddenly   21.___
    drops to half speed.
    The PROBABLE cause is
    A. the stator field is shorted
    B. a rotor winding shorted due to centrifugal force
    C. a rotor lead disconnected due to centrifugal force
    D. two rotor leads rubbing against each other

22. Of the following types of motors, the one that requires   22.___
    both A.C. and D.C. for operation is the _____ motor.
    A. universal   B. compound
    C. squirrel cage   D. synchronous

23. If the D.C. field of a synchronous motor is overexcited,   23.___
    A. it will run faster
    B. it will run slower
    C. line current will be leading
    D. it will hunt

24. A starter used for a synchronous motor would be   24.___
    A. an autotransformer   B. a resistor
    C. a rotor starter   D. the star-delta type

25. A 3Ø squirrel cage motor has 12 leads because   25.___
    A. it is a 6-phase motor
    B. they are stator and rotor leads
    C. 2 parallel leads are used on each winding
    D. the windings are used in parallel or series

TEST 4

1. To reverse direction of rotation of a split-phase motor,   1.___
   you would
    A. do nothing as it cannot be done
    B. reverse the line leads
    C. reverse polarity of all windings
    D. reverse polarity of starting winding

2. To reverse a capacitor motor, you would reverse   2.___
    A. both auxiliary and main windings
    B. the line leads
    C. the condenser
    D. the auxiliary winding

3. In a capacitor motor, the condenser is connected   3.___
    A. in series with the field
    B. across the motor terminals
    C. in parallel with the starting winding
    D. in series with the starting winding

4. To reverse the direction of a repulsion-induction motor,   4.___
   you should
    A. move the brushes so they cross the pole axis
    B. interchange terminal connections
    C. reverse the starting winding
    D. change the connections to the armature

5. To reverse rotation of a shaded pole motor, you would   5.___
    A. reverse the armature leads
    B. reverse the field leads
    C. shift the brushes
    D. do nothing as the motor cannot be readily reversed

6. A split-phase motor runs hot at no load.   6.___
   The PROBABLE reason is the
      A. starting winding is open
      B. starting winding is reversed
      C. centrifugal switch is broken
      D. running winding is completely shorted

7. The difference between the operating speed and the synchro-   7.___
   nous speed of an induction machine is called the
      A. slip   B. phase
      C. acceleration   D. frequency

8. The speed, in R.P.M., of a 10-pole, 60 cycle, 3Ø alternator   8.___
   is MOST NEARLY
      A. 3600   B. 4800   C. 1440   D. 720

9. A 2300 volt 80% PF, 60 cycle, 8-pole synchronous motor may   9.___
   be DIRECTLY connected to a pump designed for a speed of
   _____ RPM.
      A. 600   B. 900   C. 1200   D. 1800

10. The rated speed of a three-phase, 4-pole squirrel cage,   10.___
    60 cycle motor is MOST NEARLY _____ RPM.
      A. 900   B. 1200   C. 1750   D. 1800

11. The synchronous speed of a 4-pole, 25 cycle motor is   11.___
      A. 750 RPM   B. 375 RPM   C. 3750 RPM   D. not fixed

12. Three and four way switches are connected   12.___
      A. in series with the line B. across the line
      C. to the neutral   D. only loads less than 5 amps

13. Travelers are distinguished by being   13.___
      A. not connected to a current consuming device
      B. connected to one hot line
      C. connected to a current consuming device
      D. connected to a grounded line

14. Of the following types of single phase induction motors,   14.___
    the one that produces the HIGHEST starting torque is by
    the _____ method.
      A. shaded pole   B. repulsion start
      C. resistance split phase   D. capacitor split phase

15. The break down torque will vary on a squirrel cage induc-   15.___
    tion motor with a given slip _____ the voltage.
      A. inversely with   B. with the square of
      C. with the   D. with the square root of

16. A 95% efficient transformer supplies a 114 KW load.   16.___
    The input is _____ KW.
      A. 5.7   B. 108   C. 114   D. 120

17. A D.C. motor that takes 40 amperes at 250 volts delivers   17.____
    10 horsepower.
    The efficiency of this motor is APPROXIMATELY
       A. 55%   B. 64%   C. 75%   D. 100%

18. A 5 HP 220 volt D.C. motor that has an efficiency of 90%   18.____
    takes a full load current of APPROXIMATELY _____ amps.
       A. 14.3   B. 17   C. 18.8   D. 20.5

19. A 20 HP D.C. motor is 85% efficient.   19.____
    The power, in kilowatts, that it will take from the line
    is
       A. 12.7   B. 17.5   C. 20.0   D. 23.5

20. The current taken by a 1 HP 120 volt single-phase induc-   20.____
    tion motor whose efficiency is 90% and power factor of 0.8
    is _____ amps.
       A. 6.9   B. 7.8   C. 8.6   D. 6.2

21. If electricity costs 3¢ per KWH, what is the cost of   21.____
    running a 440 volt 3Ø 10 HP motor whose efficiency is
    80% for one hour?
       A. 3¢   B. 18¢   C. 22¢   D. 28¢

22. Three motor control start-stop pushbutton stations are   22.____
    connected
       A. in series   B. in parallel
       C. three way   D. in series-parallel

23. The torque of a D.C. shunt motor varies as the _____   23.____
       A. armature current
       B. cube of armature current
       C. field current squared
       D. square of the armature current

24. For fast stopping, a braking method sometimes utilizes a   24.____
    motor as a generator to create a retarding force.
    This method is known as
       A. magnetic braking   B. dynamic braking
       C. counter EMF braking   D. plugging

25. An instrument used to measure the angular speed of a motor   25.____
    is the
       A. tachometer   B. micrometer
       C. monometer   D. speedometer

11

TEST 5

1. Interpoles are
   A. connected in series with the shunt field
   B. connected in parallel with the armature
   C. used to increase the degree of compounding
   D. used to improve commutation

   1.___

2. In the D.C. shunt motor, the field
   A. has comparatively few turns of wire
   B. has comparatively many turns of wire
   C. is connected in series with the armature
   D. current is more than the line current

   2.___

3. If, in a compound motor, the series and shunt fields oppose each other, the motor
   A. is differential compound
   B. is cumulative compound
   C. will not run
   D. will overheat

   3.___

4. A cumulative compound motor has _____ set(s) of fields.
   A. 1   B. 2   C. 3   D. 4

   4.___

5. To reverse rotation of a D.C. shunt motor, you would
   A. reverse the line leads
   B. reverse the series fields
   C. reverse the armature connections
   D. shift the brushes

   5.___

6. The PROPER way to reverse the direction of rotation of a compound motor is to interchange the
   A. line leads   B. armature connections
   C. shunt field connections   D. series field connections

   6.___

7. If you attempted to start a D.C. compound motor in which the series field was open-circuited, the motor would
   A. not start   B. blow the fuse
   C. run away   D. start to reverse

   7.___

8. If the field current of a shunt motor is decreased, the motor will
   A. run away   B. run slower
   C. run faster   D. overheat

   8.___

9. To decrease the speed of a D.C. shunt wound motor below its name plate rating, it is ADVISABLE to connect
   A. resistance in the field circuit
   B. a shunt across the field circuit
   C. resistance in the armature circuit
   D. a shunt across the armature circuit

   9.___

10. The reason for using a starting box for a D.C. motor is   10.___
to
    A. reduce armature current during starting period
    B. increase the starting torque
    C. regulate the speed
    D. reduce voltage on fields during starting

11. The holding coil of a 3-point starting box is connected   11.___
    A. in series with the field
    B. in series with the line
    C. in series with the armature
    D. across the line

12. When replacing a D.C. blowout coil, it is MOST important   12.___
to
    A. have its resistance the same as the old coil
    B. have its resistance higher than the old coil
    C. see that the magnetic field reacts
    D. install it when the contacts are open

13. The usual cause of localized heating of an armature is   13.___
    A. overload
    B. eddy currents
    C. armature out of center between poles
    D. shorted armature coil

14. What would happen when a D.C. motor is running with an   14.___
open armature coil?
    A. Speed would increase.
    B. Speed would decrease.
    C. Motor would begin to spark violently.
    D. The coil would begin heating.

15. An electrical contractor files an application for inspec-   15.___
tion for a job
    A. when completed   B. when starting
    C. when half finished   D. before starting

16. Polarizing a fixture means   16.___
    A. attaching the fixture to the outlet box
    B. connecting identified conductor to shell of lampholder
    C. removing the insulation from the fixture wires
    D. connecting unidentified conductor to shell of lamp-
       holder

17. A closed circuit burglar alarm system is better than an   17.___
open circuit system because
    A. it costs less to install
    B. it gives greater protection
    C. the bell will not ring if the wire is cut
    D. it requires fewer parts

18. A portable electric drill should be grounded by means of   18.___
    A. standard attachment plug
    B. 3-prong attachment plug
    C. *T* slot attachment plug
    D. cord connector

19. A single pole switch is ALWAYS connected in the   19.___
    A. neutral leg   B. white wire
    C. identified wire   D. live leg

20. The SAFEST way for an electrician to determine whether a   20.___
    circuit is A.C. or D.C. is to
    A. use a neon test lamp
    B. test bare parts with his fingertips
    C. telephone the Edison Company
    D. use an incandescent test lamp

21. Which of the following is NOT permitted for permanent   21.___
    wiring in New York City?
    A. Armored cable (BX)   B. Rigid conduit
    C. Romex   D. EMT

22. In rigid conduit work, the GREATEST number of quarter   22.___
    bends (90°) permitted between outlets is
    A. two   B. four   C. six   D. eight

23. The standard network system used for light and power in   23.___
    New York City is
    A. 110/220 volt single phase
    B. 220 volt 2 phase 3 wire
    C. 208/120 volt 3 phase 4 wire
    D. 120/240 volt single phase 3 wire

24. The SMALLEST size service entrance conductor permitted is   24.___
    A. #2   B. #4   C. #6   D. #8

25. The ampere rating of service switches must be AT LEAST   25.___
    _____ amperes.
    A. 60   B. 30   C. 200   D. 100

_____

14

KEY (CORRECT ANSWERS)

TEST 1	TEST 2	TEST 3	TEST 4	TEST 5
1. D	1. C	1. C	1. D	1. D
2. B	2. D	2. D	2. D	2. B
3. D	3. B	3. A	3. D	3. A
4. B	4. A	4. A	4. A	4. B
5. B	5. B	5. D	5. D	5. C
6. B	6. C	6. B	6. C	6. B
7. B	7. A	7. D	7. A	7. A
8. C	8. A	8. B	8. D	8. C
9. D	9. D	9. B	9. B	9. C
10. B	10. A	10. C	10. C	10. A
11. C	11. B	11. A	11. A	11. A
12. A	12. B	12. D	12. A	12. D
13. D	13. B	13. A	13. A	13. D
14. A	14. D	14. D	14. A	14. C
15. D	15. C	15. D	15. B	15. D
16. C	16. C	16. A	16. D	16. B
17. C	17. D	17. A	17. C	17. B
18. B	18. C	18. D	18. C	18. B
19. B	19. B	19. A	19. B	19. C
20. C	20. D	20. B	20. C	20. A
21. C	21. A	21. C	21. D	21. C
22. A	22. B	22. D	22. D	22. B
23. B	23. D	23. C	23. A	23. C
24. A	24. B	24. A	24. B	24. A
25. B	25. B	25. D	25. A	25. D

EXAMINATION SECTION
TEST 1

DIRECTIONS: Each question or incomplete statement is followed by several suggested answers or completions. Select the one that BEST answers the question or completes the statement. *PRINT THE LETTER OF THE CORRECT ANSWER IN THE SPACE AT THE RIGHT.*

1. A piece of No. 1/0 emery cloth should be used to sand the commutator of a D.C. dynamo   1.____

    A. when there is sparking at the brushes
    B. under no conditions
    C. when the commutator has a "chocolate" color
    D. only when the commutator has ridges

2. Compound D.C. generators connected in parallel are *generally* provided with   2.____

    A. 3 brushes   B. an equalizer
    C. no voltage relays   D. armature resistors

3. As compared with other types of A.C. motors, the advantage of the squirrel cage motor lies in its   3.____

    A. high starting torque   B. high power factor
    C. constant speed   D. simplicity

4. A counter E.M.F. starter is so named because   4.____

    A. the accelerating contactor has a high counter E.M.F.
    B. the accelerating relay depends upon the armature terminal voltage for operation
    C. it is used only on motors that build up a high C.E.M.F.
    D. it stops the motor by means of C.E.M.F.

5. There shall NOT be more than _____ quarter bends or their equivalent from outlet to outlet in rigid conduit.   5.____

    A. 3   B. 4   C. 5   D. 6

6. Armored cable may be imbedded in masonry in buildings under construction *provided*   6.____

    A. it is type AC   B. it is fastened securely
    C. it is type ACL   D. special permission is obtained

7. An armature core is laminated in order to reduce   7.____

    A. hysteresis loss   B. eddy current loss
    C. hysteresis and eddy current loss   D. impedance loss

8. The MOST efficient size of the "white" fluorescent lamps is   8.____

    A. 15 watts   B. 30 watts   C. 40 watts   D. 100 watts

9. Condensers are placed in parallel with fluorescent glow switches in order to   9.____

    A. reduce radio interference   B. reduce the arc
    C. compensate the power factor   D. increase the lamp life

10. The SMALLEST size wire that may be used on fire alarm systems is No. _____

    A. 18   B. 16   C. 14   D. 12

11. Under the National Electric Code, a 3-way switch is classified as a(n)

    A. single pole switch   B. double pole switch
    C. 3-way switch   D. electrolier switch

12. A capacitor start-and-run motor may be reversed by reversing the

    A. running and starting capacitor leads
    B. main winding leads
    C. line leads
    D. centrifugal switch leads

13. Opening a series field circuit while a compound motor is operating, will cause

    A. the motor to stop   B. no noticeable change
    C. the motor to race   D. the motor to slow down

14. Transformers for neon signs shall have a secondary voltage NOT exceeding

    A. 10,000 volts   B. 15,000 volts
    C. 20,000 volts   D. 25,000 volts

15. A capacitor of 10 ohms reactance and zero ohms resistance is connected in series with an inductance of 7 ohms reactance and 4 ohms resistance. The total impedance is

    A. 5 ohms   B. 7 ohms   C. 17 ohms   D. 21 ohms

16. The BEST way to start a large shunt motor is with a

    A. strong field   B. weak field
    C. rheostat in series with the armature and the field
    D. starting compensator.

17. If an A.C. motor draws 50 amps., full load, the thermal cutout should be set at

    A. 75 amps.   B. 50 amps.   C. 62.5 amps.   D. 75 amps.

18. Using 1:1 ratio transformers at a given primary voltage, the HIGHEST secondary voltage may be obtained by connecting them

    A. Wye primary and Delta secondary
    B. Delta primary and Delta secondary
    C. Wye primary and Wye secondary
    D. Delta primary and Wye secondary

19. In an A.C. fire alarm system, the number of gongs allowed on a circuit is

    A. 10   B. 12   C. 14   D. 20

20. Appliance branch circuit wires shall be NO smaller than No.

    A. 8   B. 10   C. 12   D. 14

21. A current of 2 amperes in a resistor of 10 ohms will use electrical energy at the rate of _____ watts. 21._____

    A. 10   B. 20   C. 40   D. 80

22. 20-, 40-, and 50-ohm resistances are connected in series across a 110-volt D.C. supply; the current through the 20-ohm resistance is 22._____

    A. 5.5 amperes   B. 1 ampere   C. 2.2 ampers   D. 2.75 amperes

23. An electric circuit has four resistances of 20,6,30, and 12 ohms in parallel with each other. The combined resistance, in ohms, is 23._____

    A. 300   B. 30   C. 3   D. .3

24. The load for general illumination in apartment and multifamily dwellings is based on 24._____

    A. 1 1/2 watts per square foot of floor area
    B. 2 watts per square foot of floor area
    C. 3 watts per square foot of floor area
    D. 4 watts per square foot of floor area

25. Ventilation of battery rooms is necessary to 25._____

    A. keep the batteries cool
    B. prevent accumulation of explosive gases
    C. prevent deterioration of insulation
    D. supply oxygen to the room

KEYS (CORRECT ANSWERS)

1. B	11. A		
2. B	12. B		
3. D	13. A		
4. B	14. B		
5. B	15. A		
6. C	16. A		
7. B	17. C		
8. C	18. D		
9. A	19. A		
10. C	20. C		

21. B
22. B
23. C
24. B
25. B

TEST 2

DIRECTIONS: Each question or incomplete statement is followed by several suggested answers or completions. Select the one that BEST answers the question or completes the statement. *PRINT THE LETTER OF THE CORRECT ANSWER IN THE SPACE AT THE RIGHT.*

1. Dynamic braking is obtained in a motor by means of

    A. a magnetic brake
    B. a resistance connected across the armature after the current is disconnected
    C. reversing the armature
    D. reversing the field

2. The reason for using flux when soldering splices is to

    A. lower the melting point of the solder
    B. cause the joint to heat rapidly
    C. reduce the oxide on the wires
    D. prevent corrosion of the wires after soldering

3. A good ammeter should have

    A. very high resistance   B. very low resistance
    C. low resistance   D. high resistance

4. A good voltmeter should have

    A. very high resistance   B. very low resistance
    C. low resistance   D. high resistance

5. The MOST efficient type of polyphase motor to install for a large, slow speed, direct connected machine would be a

    A. wound rotor induction motor
    B. squirrel cage induction motor
    C. synchronous motor
    D. high torque induction motor

6. Mercury is added to the gas in a neon tube in order to produce the color

    A. gold   B. blue   C. white   D. red

7. An electromotive force will be built up in a conductor if it is moving

    A. in the same direction as magnetic lines of force
    B. in the opposite direction
    C. at right angles to the lines of force
    D. in any direction

8. The BEST choice of an A.C. motor to produce a high starting torque would be a

    A. synchronous motor   B. split phase motor
    C. shaded pole motor   D. wound rotor induction motor

9. The speed of a squirrel cage motor may be reduced by   9._____

   A. inserting a line resistance
   B. inserting a line reactance
   C. increasing the number of poles
   D. decreasing the number of poles

10. Three-point starting boxes provide for   10._____

   A. speed regulation   B. no field release
   C. no voltage release   D. phase reversal

11. If the #10 wire feeding a circuit were replaced with a #7 wire, the voltage drop would be reduced, *approximately,*   11._____

   A. 100%   B. 33%   C. 66%   D. 50%

12. Theatre footlight and border light branch circuits shall be so wired that in NO case will they carry *more than* _____ amperes.   12._____

   A. 10   B. 14   C. 20   D. 25

13. Which of the following is the outstanding feature of the Edison storage battery?   13._____

   A. A continued short circuit will not ruin the battery
   B. The lead plates are smaller
   C. It has a greater voltage output per cell
   D. It is less expensive than the automobile lead storage battery

14. An impedance coil is connected into a telephone circuit in the   14._____

   A. ringing circuit   B. talking circuit
   C. ringing and talking circuit
   D. secondary side of the induction coil

15. An electro reset annunciator has   15._____

   A. two coils per figure   B. one coil per figure
   C. one coil and one permanent magnet   D. manual reset arrangement

16. Locking relays may be used in   16._____

   A. open circuit burglar alarm systems only
   B. closed circuit burglar alarm systems only
   C. any type of burglar alarm system
   D. no burglar alarm system

17. The unit or electrical inductance is the   17._____

   A. henry   B. farad   C. joule   D. mho

18. The method used in calculating the total of resistances in series is NEAREST to that used in calculating   18._____

   A. condensers in series   B. inductances in parallel
   C. condensers in parallel   D. impedances in parallel

19. If 36,000 joules of work produce 5 amperes of current between two points for 60 seconds, what is the difference of potential between the two points, in volts?

    A. 600   B. 400   C. 120   D. 100

20. To measure a circuit current of 300 amps with a 100 amp ammeter, the shunt MUST have a MINIMUM capacity of _____ amps.

    A. 100   B. 200   C. 300   D. 400

21. A D.C. motor field coil connected first across a D.C. line and then across an A.C. line of equal voltage, will draw

    A. more current on D.C. than A.C.
    B. less current on D.C. than A.C.
    C. the same current on D.C. as on A.C.
    D. no current on A.C.

22. The single phase A.C. motor that produces the WEAKEST starting torque is the

    A. series A.C. motor   B. repulsion motor
    C. split phase motor   D. shaded pole motor

23. The D.C. generator whose terminal voltage falls off MOST rapidly when loaded is the_____ type.

    A. shunt   B. flat-compounded
    C. over-compounded   D. series

24. The E.M.F. produced by a primary cell depends on the

    A. size of the elements   B. amount of electrolyte
    C. distance between the elements
    D. materials used for the elements

25. A D.C. circuit consisting of 5 lamps in parallel draws 5 amperes; the current in *each* lamp is

    A. 1 ampere   B. 5 amperes
    C. determined by the resistance of the lamp
    D. 1/5 of an ampere

KEY (CORRECT ANSWERS)

1.	B		11.	D
2.	C		12.	B
3.	B		13.	A
4.	A		14.	B
5.	C		15.	A
6.	B		16.	C
7.	C		17.	A
8.	D		18.	C
9.	C		19.	C
10.	B		20.	B

21.	A
22.	D
23.	A
24.	D
25.	C

TEST 3

DIRECTIONS: Each question or incomplete statement is followed by several suggested answers or completions. Select the one that BEST answers the question or completes the statement. *PRINT THE LETTER OF THE CORRECT ANSWER IN THE SPACE AT THE RIGHT.*

1. It is good practice to install a polarity reversing switch on a direct current fluorescent circuit to

   A. lessen ends blackening
   B. prevent one end from becoming dim
   C. ease starting
   D. prevent radio interference

2. A 40-watt fluorescent lamp with necessary equipment may be satisfactorily operated from a direct current source of

   A. 110 volts
   C. either voltage
   B. 220 volts
   D. corrected power factor

3. The National Electric Code provides that residential apartments be provided with receptacle outlets for *every* _____ feet of lineal wall space.

   A. 10   B. 15   C. 20   D. 25

4. If a person is rendered unconscious by an electric shock, one should break the electrical contact, call a physician, *and*

   A. make patient comfortable until physician arrives
   B. use prone-pressure method of resuscitation
   C. administer a stimulant
   D. rub patient's body to increase circulation

5. A 1 1/2" x 4" octagonal box may contain a MAXIMUM of

   A. 5 #14 conductors
   C. 8 #14 conductors
   B. 7 #14 conductors
   D. 11 #14 conductors

6. A 1 1/2" x 4" square box may contain a MAXIMUM of

   A. 5 #14 conductors
   C. 8 #14 conductors
   B. 7 #14 conductors
   D. 11 #14 conductors

7. Damaged cords for power tools should be

   A. coated with flux and covered with rubber tape
   B. repaired with insulating tape
   C. replaced
   D. shortened to remove the damaged section

8. A source of direct current connected to a vibrating bell in series with the primary of an induction coil, will cause the **secondary** coil to produce

    A. alternating current   B. direct current
    C. pulsating direct current   D. interrupted direct current

8.____

9. Switches and attachment plugs installed in garages shall be AT LEAST _____ above the floor.

    A. 1 foot   B. 2 feet   C. 3 feet, 6 inches   D. 4 feet

9.____

10. Rigid conduit used for electrical wiring is purchased in

    A. 10 feet lengths, including coupling
    B. 10 feet lengths
    C. 9'6" lengths
    D. no standard lengths

10.____

11. Switches controlling signs shall be placed

    A. at the service equipment
    B. in the office of the premises displaying the sign
    C. within sight of the sign
    D. at the main entrance to the building

11.____

12. A self-excited alternator has

    A. slip rings for the field excitation
    B. a storage battery for the field
    C. a winding connected to the commutator
    D. no coil for direct current

12.____

13. A copper wire twice the diameter of another has a carrying capacity of _____ as great.

    A. two times   B. one-half   C. four times   D. eight times

13.____

14. The resistance of a copper bus bar is

    A. directly proportional to its length
    B. inversely proportional to its length
    C. negligible
    D. higher than that of gold

14.____

15. The resistance of a conductor depends upon the material it is made of *and*

    A. its temperature   B. where it is used
    C. the ambient temperature   D. method of installation

15.____

16. The positive terminal of an unmarked lead storage battery can *often* be identified by

    A. being larger than the negative
    B. being smaller than the negative
    C. removing the filling caps and looking at the plates
    D. using a "Y" box

16.____

17. The discharge voltage of an Edison storage cell is _____ volt(s).

    A. 1   B. 1.2   C. 2   D. 6

18. Voltmeters *often* have

    A. external shunts in parallel   B. internal shunts
    C. internal resistance coils   D. low resistance shunts

19. Selsyn motors are used

    A. to operate clocks from a direct current source
    B. at repeater stations
    C. as a generator for cathode ray tubes
    D. to charge storage batteries

20. The secondary of a current transformer

    A. is always opened with a connected load
    B. is never used with meters
    C. cannot be used on alternating current
    D. should never be opened while primary is energized

21. Circline is a development in

    A. fluorescent lighting   B. raceways
    C. incandescent lighting   D. insulating material

22. Neon signs operate on

    A. low voltage-high current   B. high current-high voltage
    C. high voltage-low current   D. low voltage-low current

23. Thermo electricity can be generated by heat applied to

    A. glass between two layers of aluminum foil
    B. two dissimilar metals
    C. two similar metals
    D. two lead plates in an electrolyte

24. To determine the power in a two-phase lighting and power system, the proper formula to use would be:

    A. $KW = \dfrac{E \times I \times PF}{1000}$ B. $KW = 1.73 \times E \times I \times PF \times 1000$

    C. $KW = \dfrac{\sqrt{2} \times E \times I \times PF}{1000}$ D. $KW = \dfrac{1.42 \times E \times W \times PF}{1000}$

25. An electric toaster operating on 120 volts has a resistance (hot) of 15 ohms. The wattage of the toaster is

    A. 1200   B. 1140   C. 1080   D. 960

KEY (CORRECT ANSWERS)

1.	B	11.	C
2.	B	12.	C
3.	C	13.	C
4.	B	14.	A
5.	C	15.	A
6.	C	16.	A
7.	C	17.	B
8.	A	18.	C
9.	D	19.	B
10.	A	20.	D

21.	A
22.	C
23.	B
24.	C
25.	D

TEST 4

DIRECTIONS: Each question or incomplete statement is followed by several suggested answers or completions. Select the one that BEST answers the question or completes the statement. *PRINT THE LETTER OF THE CORRECT ANSWER IN THE SPACE AT THE RIGHT.*

1. When using lead cable, the inner radius of the bend shall be *no less than* _____ times the internal diameter of the conduit.

    A. four   B. six   C. eight   D. ten

2. A telephone hook switch is similar in operation to a

    A. strop key   B. locking type push button
    C. locking type relay   D. two circuit electrolier switch

3. The "dielectric" of a condenser is the

    A. air surrounding the condenser
    B. material separating the plates
    C. voltage impressed on the condenser
    D. lines of force established by the current

4. The depolarizing substance in the dry cell is

    A. manganese dioxide   B. ammonium chloride
    C. zinc chloride   D. lead oxide

5. The SMALLEST wattage fluorescent lamp manufactured for home use is

    A. 6   B. 8   C. 9   D. 15

6. The Carter system of connecting three-way switches for lighting

    A. will not operate lamps in parallel
    B. is not permitted under the National Electric Code
    C. will not operate when used in conjunction with a pilot light
    D. will not operate lamps in series

7. The material offering the LEAST resistance to the flow of an electric current is

    A. iron   B. aluminum   C. German silver   D. zinc

8. To replace a four-way switch, we may use the following type:

    A. Double pole snap   B. Double pole, double throw
    C. Three-circuit electrolier   D. Three-way switch

9. The LARGEST size conductor permitted in surface metal raceways is No.

    A. 10   B. 8   C. 6   D. 4

10. The energy accumulated in a storage battery is

    A. electrical   B. chemical   C. kinetic   D. mechanical

11. A strop key is MOST similar in operation to the following switch: 11._____

    A. Double pole   B. Three-way
    C. Four-way   D. Two circuit electrolier

12. Compensators are used to start motors at   12._____

    A. reduced voltage   B. reduced speed
    C. reduced load   D. increased voltage

13. A self-excited D.C. shunt generator is operating properly in clockwise rotation. If the   13._____
direction of rotation is reversed, the

    A. brush polarity will reverse
    B. field polarity will reverse
    C. generator will fail to build up voltage
    D. output voltage will be the same in magnitude

14. If the intake port on an oil burner blower were closed, the motor would   14._____

    A. slow down   B. require more current
    C. heat up   D. require less current

15. In the event of a burnout of one single-phase transformer on a 3-phase, Wye-connected   15._____
system, you can

    A. connect the remaining two in "delta"
    B. connect the remaining two "Scott"
    C. connect the remaining two "Open Wye"
    D. not connect them to obtain 3-phase with same voltage

16. The short circuited coil imbedded in the pole face of an A.C. contactor is used to   16._____

    A. blow out the arc   B. reduce residual magnetism
    C. close the contactor   D. reduce noise and vibration

17. A motor that is built for plugging service   17._____

    A. has a built-in brake
    B. helps to compensate power factor
    C. may be connected in reverse from full speed forward
    D. has built-in reduction gears

18. Eleven #14 conductors are permitted in a 1" conduit   18._____

    A. in apartment house risers   B. under all conditions
    C. at no time
    D. for conductors between a motor and its controller

19. The number of mogul sockets on a two-wire branch circuit shall NOT exceed   19._____

    A. 8   B. 7   C. 6   D. 5

20. A 1 1/2" x 3 1/4" octagonal box may contain a MAXIMUM of   20._____

    A. 5 #14 conductors   B. 7 #14 conductors
    C. 8 #14 conductors   D. 11 #14 conductors

21. The average value of an alternating current is equal to its MAXIMUM value *times*   21

    A. 1.7232   B. .707   C. .636   D. 1.41

22. In a D.C. fire alarm system, the number of gongs allowed on a circuit is   22

    A. 10   B. 12   C. 13   D. 20

23. If the total resistance of the wire wound on a bipolar armature is 2 ohms, the armature   23
resistance is _____ ohm(s).

    A. 1   B. 2   C. 1/2   D. 4

24. Increasing the field excitation of a synchronous motor will cause the   24

    A. motor to speed up   B. motor to slow down
    C. current to lead   D. voltage to lead

25. Mercury rectifiers have   25

    A. mercury anodes   B. the positive terminal at the cathode
    C. high tank pressure   D. one anode always

KEY (CORRECT ANSWERS)

1.	D		11.	B
2.	A		12.	A
3.	B		13.	C
4.	A		14.	C
5.	A		15.	C
6.	B		16.	B
7.	B		17.	C
8.	B		18.	D
9.	C		19.	B
10.	B		20.	C

21. C
22. C
23. C
24. B
25. C

ELECTRICITY
EXAMINATION SECTION
TEST 1

DIRECTIONS: Each question or incomplete statement is followed by several suggested answers or completions. Select the one that BEST answers the question or completes the statement. *PRINT THE LETTER OF THE CORRECT ANSWER IN THE SPACE AT THE RIGHT.*

1. A prony brake is used to determine the   1.____

    A. output of a generator   B. output of a transformer
    C. horsepower output of a motor   D. input to a motor

2. The direction of rotation of a shunt motor may be reversed by   2.____

    A. reversing the line wires
    B. reversing the shunt field leads
    C. reversing the residual magnetism
    D. placing the brushes on the neutral axis

3. The torque of a series motor varies   3.____

    A. *directly* with the current on the line
    B. *inversely* with the current in the field
    C. *directly* with the current in the armature squared
    D. *inversely* with the armature current squared

4. A no-field release is *generally* found in a   4.____

    A. three-point starting box   B. four-point starting box
    C. magnetic switch   D. thermal cut-out

5. No voltage release is *generally* provided for   5.____

    A. in a three-point starter   B. in a magnetic circuit breaker
    C. across the line starter   D. in a four-point starter

6. A. D.C. 150-volt voltmeter whose resistance is 15,000 ohms may be used to read 300 volts by connecting a resistance in series whose value is   6.____

    A. 1,500 ohms   B. 30,000 ohms   C. 3,000 ohms   D. 15,000 ohms

7. The horsepower of a D.C. motor is equal to   7.____

    A. $E \times I$ B. $E \times I \times EFF$ C. $\dfrac{E \times I}{746}$ D. $\dfrac{E \times I \times EFF}{746}$

8. As the speed increases, the back e.m.f. of a shunt motor   8.____

    A. *decreases* the current taken by the motor
    B. *increases* until it equals the line voltage
    C. *does not change*
    D. *decreases*

9. Split phase starting in single phase motor is used to

    A. divide the current equally between two circuits
    B. double the speed of the motor
    C. decrease the torque of the motor
    D. produce a rotating field

10. Capacitor motors are *usually* preferred to other single phase motors because of

    A. better speed regulation   B. easy speed control
    C. higher starting power factor   D. easier maintenance

11. A split phase induction motor is reversed by reversing the

    A. line wires   B. starting winding
    C. starting and running windings   D. rotor

12. The speed of a synchronous motor

    A. *increases* when the field current increases
    B. *decreases* when the field current increases
    C. *remains constant*
    D. *increases* when the field current decreases

13. The horsepower of a one horsepower single-phase motor whose efficiency is 90% is

    A. .9 H.P.   B. 1 H.P.   C. 1.1 B.P.   D. 1.8 H.P.

14. The output line voltage of three 208-volt, 1:1 transformers, connected wye-primary, delta-secondary, across a three-phase 208-volt line, is

    A. 208 volts   B. 240 volts   C. 60 volts   D. 120 volts

15. The output line voltage of three 208-volt, 1:1 transformers, connected delta-wye across a 208-volt line, is

    A. $120 \sqrt{3}$ volts   B. 240 volts   C. 208 volts   D. $208 \sqrt{3}$ volts

16. The output line voltage of three 120-volt, 1:2 transformers, connected delta-delta across a 120-volt line, is

    A. 120 volts   B. 240 volts   C. $120 \sqrt{3}$ volts   D. $240 \sqrt{3}$ volts

17. Potential transformers are used to

    A. *increase* the voltage output of a line
    B. *decrease* the voltage of the line to a safe value
    C. *decrease* the line voltage to a safe value for use with a voltmeter
    D. *regulate* the line voltage

18. Low power factor in an induction motor   18.____

    A. *increases* the current drawn by the motor
    B. *increases* the efficiency
    C. *reduces* the speed considerably
    D. *increases* the torque of the motor

19. The rotation of a three-phase induction motor is *reversed* by reversing   19.____

    A. all the line wires   B. any two leads
    C. the motor   D. the field connections

20. The *true* power of a three-phase load is   20.____

    A. $3 \times E \times I$ B. $\sqrt{3} \times E \times I \times$ Efficiency

    C. $\dfrac{3E \times I \times EFF \times \text{Power Factory}}{746}$ D. $\dfrac{\sqrt{3}E \times I \times EFF \times PF}{746}$

21. A 6-pole, 208-volt, synchronous motor connected to a 60-cycle line has a speed of   21.____

    A. 1800 R.P.M.   B. 3600 R.P.M.   C. 1200 R.P.M.   D. 900 R.P.M.

22. Series A.C. motors have a speed which   22.____

    A. is constant
    B   varies inversely with the load
    C. is controlled by a field rheostat
    D. is controlled by magnetic switches

23. Compensators are used to start motors at   23.____

    A. reduced voltage   B. reduced speed
    C. reduced load   D. maximum load

24. To obtain minimum speed, the field rheostat of a shunt motor MUST be set so that its   24.____
resistance is

    A. minimum   B. one-fourth of maximum
    C. one-half of maximum   D. maximum

25. The power factor of single-phase induction motors may be *improved* by   25.____

    A. splitting the phase
    B. using shaded poles
    C. using condensers
    D. increasing the air gap between the rotor and the field windings

KEY (CORRECT ANSWERS)

1.	C		11.	B
2.	B		12.	C
3.	C		13.	B
4.	A		14.	D
5.	D		15.	D
6.	D		16.	B
7.	D		17.	C
8.	A		18.	A
9.	D		19.	B
10.	C		20.	D

21.	C
22.	B
23.	A
24.	A
25.	C

TEST 2

DIRECTIONS: Each question or incomplete statement is followed by several suggested answers or completions. Select the one that BEST answers the question or completes the statement. *PRINT THE LETTER OF THE CORRECT ANSWER IN THE SPACE AT THE RIGHT.*

1. The power output of a three-phase generator may be determined by

    1.____

    A. a watt meter and a voltmeter   B. two wattmeters
    C. a prony brake   D. a three-phase watthourmeter

2. When load is added to a D.C. motor with interpoles, the brushes are

    2.____

    A. shifted in the direction of rotation
    B. shifted in the direction opposite that of rotation
    C. placed at the neutral axis
    D. left in the same position

3. The current in the series field of a compound D.C. generator

    3.____

    A. *increases* if the speed is increased
    B. *decreases* as load is added
    C. *decreases* as speed increases
    D. *increases* as load is added

4. A voltmeter may be used to measure

    4.____

    A. low resistances
    B. the resistance of a motor armature
    C. the resistance of a series field
    D. the insulation resistance of a D.C. field

5. Ammeter shunts are used to

    5.____

    A. increase the current through the ammeter coil
    B. supply a path of low resistance for the flow of current
    C. divide the current evenly between the instrument and the shunt
    D. reduce the error of the reading

6. Watthourmeters measure

    6.____

    A. power   B. volts x amperes
    C. energy   D. time

7. If the constant of a wattmeter is 4, the *actual* power is

    7.____

    A. $\frac{1}{4}$ the reading   B. 4 times the reading

    C. $\sqrt{4}$ times the reading   D. $\frac{1}{4}$ E x I

8. A cumulatively connected compound motor has the series field connected so that its magnetic field

    A.   assists the shunt field   B.   opposes the shunt field
    C.   compensates for the I.R. drop of the line
    D.   reduces sparking

9. A three-phase, 4-wire, 208-volt distribution system supplies

    A.   120 volts   B.   208 and 104 volts
    C.   208 and $\sqrt{3}$ x 208 volts   D.   208 volts and $\sqrt{3}$ x 104 volts

10. The armature resistance of a 120-volt D.C. motor is .05 ohms. At normal speed it draws 20 amperes.
The back e.m.f. at normal speed is

    A.   1 volt   B.   20 volts   C.   119 volts   D.   6 volts

11. The reactance of a field coil whose inductance is 0.1 henry when connected to a 60-cycle source of power, is

    A.   377 ohms   B.   3.77 ohms   C.   37.7 ohms   D.   3770 ohms

12. The speed regulation of a shunt motor *as compared to* that of a cumulative compound motor is

    A.   poorer   B.   the same   C.   better   D.   much poorer

13. As the load of a squirrel cage motor is increased to full rated load, its power factor

    A.   increases   B.   remains unchanged
    C.   decreases a little   D.   decreases considerably

14. When load is added to a compound generator whose series field bucks the shunt field,

    A.   its speed will increase
    B.   the terminal voltage will rise
    C.   voltage control will be impossible
    D.   the terminal voltage will decrease

15. The number of pairs of poles in a 25-cycle generator revolving at 750 R.P.M. is

    A.   2   B.   3   C.   1   D.   4

16. The grid in a triode radio tube controls the

    A.   plate voltage   B.   flow of current in the plate circuit
    C.   grid voltage   D.   filament voltage

17. A microampere is equivalent to

    A.   1,000,000 amperes   B.   .0000001 ampere
    C.   .001 ampere   D.   1,000 amperes

18. In radio, a continuous wave has   18.____

    A.   equal amplitude for all cycles
    B.   decreasing amplitude for each cycle
    C.   a mixed amplitude
    D.   a rising amplitude for each cycle

19. A microphone changes   19.____

    A.   electrical current into sound
    B.   the value of the current
    C.   sound to electrical current
    D.   the volume of the output

20. The photo-electric cell used for the sound system of motion picture machines *changes*   20.____

    A.   sound into electrical energy
    B.   light into sound
    C.   light waves into electrical current
    D.   sound waves into light

21. The resistance of a conductor   21.____

    A.   depends upon the type of insulation
    B.   is directly proportional to its length
    C.   is changed with its method of installation
    D.   is immaterial when asbestos insulation is used

22. The material offering the LEAST resistance to the flow of an electric current is   22.____

    A. gold   B. aluminum   C. silver   D. copper

23. The window of a 30 amp. plug fuse is   23.____

    A. hexagonal   B. octagonal   C. round   D. irregular

24. The MAXIMUM voltage permitted for type "R" wire is   24.____

    A. 300   B. 500   C. 600   D. 1000

25. The SMALLEST size wire permitted for fixture wiring is number   25.____

    A. 14   B. 16   C. 18   D. 20

KEY (CORRECT ANSWERS)

1.	B		11.	C
2.	D		12.	C
3.	D		13.	A
4.	D		14.	D
5.	B		15.	A
6.	C		16.	B
7.	B		17.	B
8.	A		18.	A
9.	A		19.	C
10.	C		20.	C

21.	B
22.	C
23.	C
24.	C
25.	C

———

TEST 3

DIRECTIONS: Each question or incomplete statement is followed by several suggested answers or completions. Select the one that BEST answers the question or completes the statement. *PRINT THE LETTER OF THE CORRECT ANSWER IN THE SPACE AT THE RIGHT.*

1. In splicing solid duplex wire, the splice should be   1.____

   A. staggered   B. bunched   C. interwoven   D. tapered

2. Type SNA conductors are permitted in   2.____

   A. new installations only
   B. rewiring where space is not available in existing raceways
   C. old and new installations
   D. switchboard wiring only

3. A McIntire sleeve is *generally* used   3.____

   A. in hanging fixtures   D. to insulate splices
   C. as an aid in bending conduit   D. in splicing aerial wires

4. The code states that solderless conductors may   4.____

   A. not be used   B. be used
   C. be used with special permission only
   D. be used only for fixture splicing

5. The reason for using flux when soldering splices is to   5.____

   A. lower the melting point of the solder
   B. cause the joint to heat rapidly
   C. reduce the oxide on the wires
   D. prevent corrosion of the wires

6. If a person is rendered unconscious by an electric shock, one should break the electrical contact, call a physician, *and*   6.____

   A. make patient comfortable until physician arrives
   B. use prone-pressure method of resuscitation
   C. administer a stimulant
   D. rub patient's body to increase circulation

7. The hydrometer is used to measure   7.____

   A. specific gravity of liquids
   B. specific gravity of solids
   C. water pressure in motor-driven pumps
   D. the amount of water passing a given point in a given time

8. The voltage of a fully-charged lead storage cell is   8.____

   A. 1.5   B. 2.2   C. 1.25   D. 6

9. In a dry cell, manganese dioxide is used

    A. as an electrolyte   B. to remove the hydrogen
    C. to generate hydrogen
    D. to prevent leakage through the zinc

10. Eddy currents can be reduced by

    A. using alternating current
    B. increasing the voltage
    C. using rubber mounts under solenoids
    D. laminating the magnetic circuit

11. A four-way switch can be substituted for a

    A. 3-circuit electrolier switch   B. double pole snap switch
    C. 3-way switch   D. 4-circuit electrolier switch

12. A synchroscope is used to

    A. parallel alternators   B. measure efficiency
    C. view fast-moving objects   D. check X-ray tubes

13. A Wheatstone bridge is in balance when the galvanometer needle reads

    A. zero   B. 100   C. 500   D. 1000

14. Insulation resistance is *generally* measured by a

    A. megger   B. magneto   C. trailer   D. bell and battery

15. The bleck system refers to

    A. connectors for neutral grids
    B. a railroad signal system
    C. a system of wiring radio networks
    D. transformer supply to isolated plants

16. In fluorescent lighting, the elements at each end of the tube are known as

    A. electrodes   B. chokes   C. ballasts   D. tubulations

17. In place of a starter on a fluorescent fixture, one can use a

    A. capacitator   B. momentary contact switch
    C. condenser   D. reactor

18. The method used in wiring the component luminous tubings in neon signs is

    A. series   B. parallel   C. series or parallel
    D. series parallel

19. Two small spheres of equal diameter have charges of 1.6×10^{-4} coulombs and 4.0×10^{-6} coulombs, respectively.
    If the centers of the spheres are spaced 0.4 meters apart, the electrical force existing between the two spheres in newtons is

    A. 3.6×10^{1} B. 2.8×10^{-7} C. 3.0×10^{-8} D. 2.75×10^{4}

20. Switches controlling signs shall be placed 20.____

    A. at the service equipment
    B. within sight of the sign
    C. at the main entrance to the building
    D. in the office of the premises displaying the sign

21. A type "S" fuse is rated from 21.____

    A. 0-30 amps.   B. 30-60 amps.
    C. 60-100 amps.   D. over 500 volts

22. A 220-110 volt service feeds a lighting panel. Trouble has occurred which has caused the 22.____
    incandescent lights to burn dimly.
    The MOST probable cause is

    A. a blown fuse on one line leg   B. poor quality of the lamps
    C. 100% power factor   D. an open neutral factor

23. In charging Edison-type storage batteries, the two leads from the charger, marked plus 23.____
    and minus, respectively, are connected to the battery as follows:

    A. 1 minus lead to minus terminal, plus lead to plus terminal
    B. Minus lead to plus terminal, plus lead to minus terminal
    C. By interchanging the polarity
    D. As indicated on the nameplate on the charger, since chargers differ

24. The energy accumulated in a storage battery is 24.____

    A. electrical   B. chemical   C. kinetic   D. mechanical

25. Appliance branch circuit wires shall be no smaller than number 25.____

    A. 8   B. 10   C. 12   D. 14

KEY (CORRECT ANSWERS)

1.	A	11.	C
2.	D	12.	A
3.	D	13.	A
4.	B	14.	A
5.	C	15.	B
6.	B	16.	A
7.	A	17.	B
8.	B	18.	A
9.	B	19.	A
10.	D	20.	B

21.	A
22.	D
23.	A
24.	B
25.	C

———

TEST 4

DIRECTIONS: Each question or incomplete statement is followed by several suggested answers or completions. Select the one that BEST answers the question or completes the statement. *PRINT THE LETTER OF THE CORRECT ANSWER IN THE SPACE AT THE RIGHT.*

1. Portable cords for stage lighting shall be of the type known as

    A. S   B. SN   C. R   D. VC

    1._____

2. The switch for the emergency lights of a theatre shall be located

    A. at the stage switchboard   B. in the manager's office
    C. in the projection booth   D. in the lobby

    2._____

3. The purpose of bombarding a neon tube is to

    A. remove inpurities   B. remove the tubulation
    C. test the tube   D. provide space for the electrodes

    3._____

4. To find the impedance in an inductive circuit, it is necessary to use the formula,

    A. $Z = 2\pi fl$ B. $Z = \sqrt{R^2 \times W}$

    C. $Z = \sqrt{R^2 + (2\pi fl)^2}$ D. $Z = \sqrt{3} \times E \times I \times PF$

    4._____

5. An electro-magnet connected to a source of direct current will have

    A. resistance   B. inductive reactance
    C. capacitative reactance   D. impedance

    5._____

6. The formula which will give an answer in watts is

    A. $\dfrac{HP \times 746}{E \times I \times EFF}$ B. $\sqrt{3} \times E \times I \times PF$

    C. $2\pi FL$ D. $\dfrac{E}{I} \times EFF$

    6._____

7. A vibrating bell can be changed into a single stroke bell by

    A. connecting a conductor from contact point to the grounded binding post
    B. adjusting the contact point
    C. eliminating one of the coils
    D. rewinding the coils

    7._____

8. A bell ringing transformer consists of

    A. two coils
    B. two coils and an iron core
    C. two coils of different-size wires and an iron core
    D. two coils and a metal case

    8._____

9. Bells may be operated from a D.C. lighting line

   A. by a transformer
   C. under no circumstances
   B. by use of a lamp resistance
   D. by means of a rectifier

10. A strop key is MOST similar in operation to a

    A. double pole switch
    C. 4-way switch
    B. 3-way switch
    D. 2-circuit electrolier switch

11. An electro-reset annunciator has

    A. 2 coils per figure
    C. 1 coil and 1 permanent magnet per figure
    D. a manual reset arrangement
    B. 1 coil per figure

12. Locking relays may be used in

    A. open circuit burglar alarm systems only
    B. closed circuit burglar alarm systems only
    C. any type of burglar alarm system
    D. no burglar alarm system

13. The term, high potential, designates voltages of from

    A. 301 to 600 volts
    C. 2,001 to 15,000 volts
    B. 601 to 2, 000 volts
    D. 601 to 5,000 volts

14. Under the National Electric Code, a 3-way switch is classified as a(n)

    A. single pole switch
    C. 3-way switch
    B. double pole switch
    D. electrolier switch

15. In an emergency, a 3-way switch may be replaced by a

    A. 2-circuit electrolier switch
    C. 4-way switch
    B. double pole switch
    D. 3-circuit electrolier switch

16. To replace a 4-way switch, we may use a

    A. double pole snap switch
    B. double pole double throw switch
    C. 3-circuit electrolier switch
    D. 4-way switch

17. A standard remote control switch may be operated by a

    A. single pole switch
    C. 3-way switch
    B. double pole switch
    D. momentary contact switch

18. A telephone book switch is similar in operation to a

    A. strop key
    C. locking type relay
    B. locking type push button
    D. 2-circuit electrolier switch

19. To replace a telephone transmitter, we may use a

    A. ribbon microphone
    C. condenser microphone
    B. carbon microphone
    D. velocity microphone

20. An induction coil is used in a telephone circuit to   20.____

    A. prevent high frequency current from returning to the battery
    B. increase the voltage
    C. prevent cross talk
    D. permit more than one conversation at a time

21. The MOST common type of private telephone system is   21.____

    A. common ringing - common talking
    B. selective ringing - common talking
    C. selective ringing - selective talking
    D. dial phone

22. Magnetoes as used in telephone systems   22.____

    A. supply current to the ringing circuit
    B. supply current to the talking circuit
    C. supplement the current supplied by the cells
    D. test the talking circuit

23. In connecting stranded wires under binding screws, BEST practice calls for   23.____

    A. twisting the ends and placing them under the binding screws
    B. placing the ends under the binding screws without twisting them
    C. twisting the ends, soldering them and placing them under the binding screw in the
        direction the screw tends to tighten
    D. soldering the strands and tightening under the binding screw in a counter-clock-
        wise direction

24. A 600-volt cartridge fuse may be recognized by its   24.____

    A. blue label   B. green label
    C. red label   D. brown label

25. A plug fuse of less than 15 amperes may be recognized by its   25.____

    A. hexagonal window opening   B. round window opening
    C. square window opening   D. octagonal window opening

──────────

KEY (CORRECT ANSWERS)

1.	A	11.	A
2.	D	12.	C
3.	A	13.	D
4.	C	14.	A
5.	A	15.	C
6.	B	16.	B
7.	A	17.	D
8.	C	18.	A
9.	B	19.	B
10.	B	20.	B

21.	B
22.	A
23.	C
24.	C
25.	A

EXAMINATION SECTION
TEST 1

DIRECTIONS: Each question or incomplete statement is followed by several suggested answers or completions. Select the one that BEST answers the question or completes the statement. *PRINT THE LETTER OF THE CORRECT ANSWER IN THE SPACE AT THE RIGHT.*

1. For a given level of illumination, the cost of electrical energy with fluorescent lighting fixtures as compared with incandescent lighting fixtures is

    A. less   B. the same
    C. more   D. dependent on the utility rate

1.____

2. The Initial current of an Incandescent lamp (tungsten) as compared with Its normal operating current is

    A. less
    B. the same
    C. more
    D. dependent on the system frequency

2.____

3. According to the electrical code, fixtures in which the wiring may be exposed to temperatures in excess of 110° F (60° C)

    A. are prohibited
    B. shall be wired with type AF fixture wires
    C. shall be so designed or ventilated and installed to operate at temperatures which will not cause deterioration of the wiring
    D. shall have suitable thermal insulation between the fixture and any adjacent combustible material

3.____

4. The direction of rotation of a d.c. shunt motor can be reversed by

    A. reversing the line terminals
    B. reversing the field and armature
    C. reversing the field or armature
    D. flashing the field

4.____

5. A starting device which will limit the starting current of a d.c. motor is generally required because

    A. the counter e.m.f. is maximum at standstill
    B. the inertia of the driven load causes excessive starting current
    C. the counter e.m.f. is zero at standstill
    D. decreased starting current increases the starting torque

5.____

6. According to the electrical code, motor disconnecting means shall be located

    A. within 10 feet of the motor
    B. within sight of the controller
    C. within 15 feet of the motor
    D. where convenient

6.____

7. According to the electrical code, the controller for an a.c. motor shall be capable of interrupting

    A. twice the full load current of the motor
    B. three times the full load current of the motor
    C. five times the full load current of the motor
    D. the stalled rotor current

8. According to the electrical code, motor disconnecting means shall have a continuous duty rating, in percent, of the name plate current rating of the motor of AT LEAST

    A. 100%   B. 115%   C. 150%   D. 200%

9. The lumens per watt taken by a lamp varies with the type and size of lamp. Given that a one candle power light source emits 12.57 lumens, the lumens per watt taken by a 75 candle power lamp drawing 40 watts is *approximately*

    A. 1.9   B. 6.7   C. 23.6   D. 240

10. A 230-volt, 25-cycle magnetic brake coil is to be rewound to operate properly on 60 cycles at the same voltage. Assuming that the coil at 25 cycles has 1800 turns, at 60 cycles the number of turns should be

    A. *reduced* to 750   B. *increased* to 2400
    C. *reduced* to 420   D. *increased* to 3000

11. Nichrome wire having a resistance of 200 ohms per 100 feet is to be used for a heater requiring a total resistance of 10 ohms.
The length, in feet, of wire required is

    A. 5   B. 15   C. 25   D. 50

12. The MAIN reason for grounding conduit is to prevent the conduit from becoming

    A. corroded by electrolysis
    B. magnetized
    C. a source of radio interference
    D. accidentally energized at a higher potential than ground

13. A feeder consisting of a positive and a negative wire supplies a motor load. The feeder is connected to bus-bars having a constant potential of 230 volts. The feeder is 500 feet long and consists of two 250,000 circular-nil conductors. The maximum load on the feeder is 170 amps. Assume that the resistance of 1000 feet of this cable is 0.0431 ohm. The voltage, at the motor terminals, is MOST NEARLY

    A. 201 V   B. 209 V   C. 213 V   D. 217 V

14. With reference to question 13 above, the efficiency of transmission, in percent, is MOST NEARLY

    A. 83%   B. 87%   C. 91%   D. 97%

15. With reference to a.c. motors, in addition to overload, many other things cause fuses to blow. The fuse will blow if, in starting an a.c. motor, the operator throws the starting switch of the compensator to the running position

A. too slowly
B. too quickly
C. with main switch in open position
D. with main switch in close position

16. A change in speed of a d.c. motor of 10 to 15 percent can USUALLY be made by   16.____

   A. rewinding the armature
   B. rewinding the field
   C. decreasing the number of turns in the field coils
   D. increasing or decreasing the gap between the armature and field

17. In order to check the number of poles in a 3-phase wound rotor induction motor, it is nec-   17.____
   essary to check the no-load speed. The no-load speed is obtained by running the motor
   with load disconnected and with the rotor resistance

   A. short-circuited   B. all in
   C. half in   D. one-third in

18. A group of industrial oil burners are equipped with several electric preheaters which can   18.____
   be used singly or in combination to heat the #6 oil for the burners. Electric preheater "A"
   alone can heat a certain quantity of oil from 70^n to 180^n in 15 minutes and preheater "B"
   alone can do the same job in 30 minutes. If both preheaters are used together, they will
   do the job in _____ minutes.

   A. 12   B. 11   C. 10   D. 9

19. With reference to armature windings, in a wave winding, regardless of the number of   19.____
   poles, ONLY _____ brushes are necessary.

   A. two   B. four   C. six   D. eight

20. The MINIMUM number of overload devices required for a 3-phase a.c. motor connected   20.____
   to a 120/208 volt, 3-phase, 4 wire system is

   A. 1   B. 2   C. 3   D. 4

21. According to the electrical code, an externally operable switch may be used as the   21.____
   starter for a motor of not over 2 horsepower (and not over 300 volts) provided it has a rating of AT LEAST

   A. 2 times the stalled rotor current of the motor
   B. 2 times the full load current of the motor
   C. 115% of the full load current of the motor
   D. 150% of the stalled rotor current of the motor

22. According to the electrical code, a single disconnecting means may serve a group of   22.____
   motors provided

   A. all motors are 1/2 HP or less
   B. all motors are within a short distance from each other
   C. all motors are located within a single room and within sight of the disconnecting
      means
   D. one-half of the motors are located within a single room and within sight of the dis-
      connecting means

23. In a 3-phase system with 3 identical loads connected in delta, if the line voltage is 4160 volts, the line to neutral voltage is

    A. indeterminate
    C. 2400 volts
    B. 7200 volts
    D. 2000 volts

24. If the current in each line is 100 amperes, the currents in each of the individual loads is (under the conditions as set forth in question 23)

    A. indeterminate
    C. 173 amps
    B. 57.7 amps
    D. 50.0 amps

25. In a 3-phase system with 3 identical loads connected in wye, if the line to neutral voltage is 115 volts, the line voltage is

    A. indeterminate
    C. 200 volts
    B. 208 volts
    D. 220 volts

26. A circuit composed of a 6-ohm resistance, a 10-ohm capacitative reactance, and an 18-ohm inductive reactance connected in series is energized by a 120 volt a.c. supply. The current, in amperes, flowing in this circuit is

    A. 0   B. 12   C. 35   D. 20

27. With reference to question 26 above, the power, in watts, used in this circuit is

    A. 0   B. 1440   C. 420   D. 864

28. With reference to question 26 above, the power factor, in percent, is

    A. 100   B. 60   C. 80   D. 90

29. With reference to question 26 above, the total impedance, in ohms, of the circuit is

    A. 10   B. 34   C. 14   D. 28

30. A triode does NOT have a

    A. cathode
    C. control grid
    B. screen grid
    D. plate

31. An industrial plant utilizes acetone as a solvent in one area. All wiring in this area must be

    A. vaportight
    C. explosionproof
    B. watertight
    D. of normal construction

32. In an area where explosionproof wiring is required, each conduit entering an enclosure containing apparatus which may produce arcs, sparks, or high temperatures shall be provided with

    A. insulating bushings
    B. a cable terminator
    C. an approved sealing compound
    D. double locknuts

33. Decreasing the bias voltage on the control grid of a triode (making it less negative with respect to the cathode) causes the plate current to   33._____

    A. not change   B. increase
    C. decrease   D. oscillate

Questions 34-46.

DIRECTIONS: The following questions 34 to 46 inclusive are to be answered in accordance with the provisions of the electrical code.

34. The MINIMUM size of wire for signalling systems is   34._____

    A. #14AWG   B. #16AWG   C. #18AWG   D. #19AWG

35. The MINIMUM size of service entrance conductors is   35._____

    A. #2AWG   B. #4AWG   C. #6AWG   D. #8AWG

36. The MAXIMUM number of individual sets of service equipment which can be supplied from one set of service entrance conductors is   36._____

    A. 1   B. 2   C. 4   D. 6

37. Service switches of ratings larger than 1,200 amperes   37._____

    A. are prohibited
    B. shall be of the pressure contact type
    C. shall be of the air circuit breaker type
    D. shall be remotely operable

38. The rating of service switches shall be less than   38._____

    A. the computed load current
    B. twice the computed load current
    C. one and a half times the computed load current
    D. one and a quarter times the computed load current

39. The allowable current carrying capacity of conductors in raceway or cable   39._____

    A. is independent of the number of conductors
    B. shall be reduced to 70% of table values if more than three conductors are contained within the raceway or cable
    C. shall be reduced to 50% of the table values if more than six conductors are contained in the raceway or cable
    D. shall be reduced to 80% for 4-6 conductors and to 70% for 7-9 conductors in the same raceway or cable

40. The MAXIMUM number of conductors for general light and power in a single raceway is   40._____

    A. 6   B. 9   C. 15   D. unlimited

41. The number of signal wires in a conductor raceway shall be

    A. the same as for lighting and power conductors
    B. such that their total cross-sectional area shall not exceed 50% of the cross-sectional area of the conduit or raceway
    C. the maximum number which can be easily installed
    D. such that their total cross-sectional area shall not exceed 40% of the cross-sectional area of the conduit or raceway

42. Lightning arrestors for receiving station antennas shall operate at a voltage of NOT more than _____ volts.

    A. 100   B. 200   C. 500   D. 1000

43. The MINIMUM size of copper ground connection to lightning arrestors for receiving antennas shall be

    A. #14AWG   B. #10AWG   C. #6AWG   D. #16AWG

44. Only motor generator sets having a generated voltage of 65 volts or less may be protected by

    A. one protective device in the generator armature circuit
    B. a protective device in each armature lead
    C. the over current protective devices in the motor circuit set to trip when the generators are delivering not more than 150% of their full load rated current
    D. the motor running protective devices of the motor

45. Single pole protective devices for direct current generators MUST be activated by

    A. the total generated current, including all field current
    B. total current except that in the shunt field
    C. separate elements in each brush lead
    D. separate elements in each line lead

46. Motor control equipment for hazardous locations MUST

    A. not produce sparks
    B. be contained in an enclosure which is vaportight
    C. be capable of withstanding an external explosion
    D. be of a type specifically approved for the installation

47. A room is 20 feet wide and is to be provided with 4 rows of lighting outlets symmetrically spaced. The distance from the wall to the center line of the first fixture row will be

    A. 5'0"   B. 10'0"   C. 7'6"   D. 2'6"

48. A fixture mounting height of 9'6" is specified for a room with a ceiling height of 12'0", utilizing fixtures with a height of 6". The size of stem required is MOST NEARLY

    A. 3'0"   B. 2'6"   C. 2'0"   D. 1'6"

49. Specifications for a project require that 40W, T-12, RS/CW lamps be installed in a given group of fixtures. The type of lamp required is   49.____

    A. 40 watt, type 12, reflector spot, clear white, incandescent
    B. 40 watt, single pin, relay start, code white, fluorescent
    C. 40 watt, bi-pin, rapid start, cool white, fluorescent
    D. type 12, medium base, recessed spot, clear white, incandescent

50. Specifications for a project require the use of indirect type of lighting fixtures. The one of the following types that will meet this requirement is   50.____

    A. RCM dome fixture
    B. concentric ring fixture with silverbowl lamp
    C. downlight with par 38 spot
    D. opal glass bowl

KEY (CORRECT ANSWERS)

1. A	11. D	21. B	31. C	41. D
2. C	12. D	22. C	32. C	42. C
3. C	13. D	23. C	33. B	43. A
4. C	14. D	24. B	34. D	44. C
5. C	15. B	25. C	35. B	45. B
6. B	16. D	26. B	36. D	46. D
7. D	17. A	27. D	37. B	47. D
8. B	18. C	28. B	38. D	48. C
9. C	19. A	29. A	39. D	49. C
10. A	20. B	30. B	40. B	50. B

TEST 2

DIRECTIONS: Each question or incomplete statement is followed by several suggested answers or completions. Select the one that BEST answers the question or completes the statement. *PRINT THE LETTER OF THE CORRECT ANSWER IN THE SPACE AT THE RIGHT.*

1. The list of symbols for the plans for a project gives and defines the following symbol:

    0_{A5C} - Incandescent lighting fixture, letters, and number indicate fixture type per specifications, circuit number and controlling switch, respectively.

    The symbol for a fixture connected to circuit 8, controlled by a switch designated "e" and conforming to the requirements of a type D fixture would be

    A. 0_{E8d} B. 0_{d8E} C. 0_{D8e} D. $0_{8eD}{}^{0}$

Questions 2-5.

DIRECTIONS: The questions numbered 2 to 5 inclusive shall be answered in accordance with the diagram which appears below.

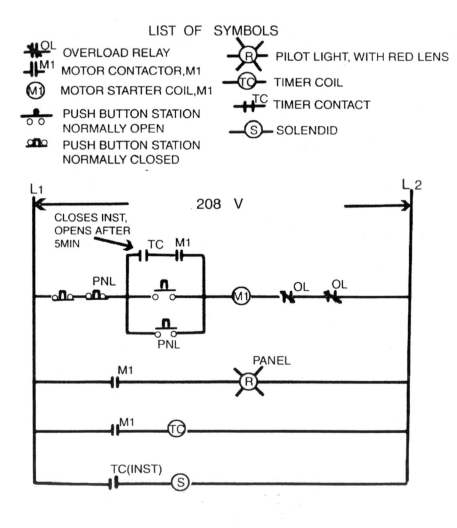

LIST OF SYMBOLS

OL OVERLOAD RELAY

M1 MOTOR CONTACTOR, M1

(M1) MOTOR STARTER COIL, M1

PUSH BUTTON STATION NORMALLY OPEN

PUSH BUTTON STATION NORMALLY CLOSED

(R) PILOT LIGHT, WITH RED LENS

(TC) TIMER COIL

TC TIMER CONTACT

(S) SOLENDID

2. The above schematic diagram indicates a desired control scheme for a pump motor. The number of locations the motor can be started from is (are)

    A. 1   B. 2   C. 3   D. 4

2.____

3. Of the following, the one which contains the most complete and correct list of possible operations which will cause the already started motor to stop is

    A. pressing of stop PB after 5 minutes have elapsed since motor started, or operation of OL
    B. a lapse of 5 minutes since starting of motor, or pressing of stop PB, or operation of OL
    C. the passing of 5 minutes from the time of starting, or pressing, of stop PB, or operation of OL, or loss of voltage
    D. loss of voltage after 5 minutes have elapsed since starting motor, or operation of OL

3.____

4. The solenoid will be energized

    A. as long as the motor starter is energized
    B. only as long as the start PB is depressed
    C. for five minutes
    D. until the stop PB is depressed

4.____

5. If the timer fails to close its associated contact, the motor

    A. cannot run
    B. will run only as long as the start PB is depressed
    C. will run continuously
    D. will run for five minutes

5.____

Questions 6-8.

DIRECTIONS: The following questions 6 to 8 inclusive should be answered in accordance with the diagram below.

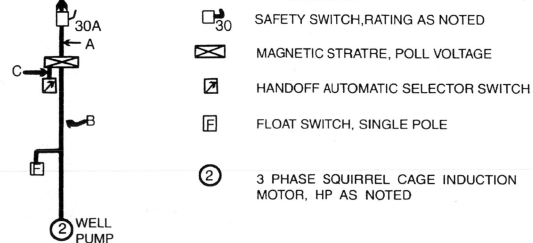

TO 208 V POWER PANEL(30)

LEGEND

30A	
← A	
C→	
↗	SAFETY SWITCH, RATING AS NOTED
	MAGNETIC STRATRE, POLL VOLTAGE
	HANDOFF AUTOMATIC SELECTOR SWITCH
B	FLOAT SWITCH, SINGLE POLE
F	
WELL PUMP	3 PHASE SQUIRREL CAGE INDUCTION MOTOR, HP AS NOTED

6. The required number of conductors at point "A" is

    A. 2   B. 3   C. 4   D. 5

7. The required number of conductors at point "B" is

    A. 2   B. 3   C. 4   D. 5

8. The required number of conductors at point "C" is

    A. 2   B. 3   C. 4   D. 5

9. The LEAST number of single-phase wattmeters that can be be used to measure the power in an unbalanced 3-phase, 4-wire a.c. circuit is

    A. 1   B. 2   C. 3   D. 4

10. A note on a plan states: "All runs shall be 3/4" conduit with 2#12AWG conductors or number of #12 conductors indicated by hatchmarks unless otherwise designated." A run is shown as follows: —/—/—/
This run consists of

    A. 2#12, 1/2"C   B. 3#12, 1/2"C
    C. 3#12, 3/4"C   D. 2#12, 3/4"C

11. Specifications for a particular project call for a system of empty conduits and outlet boxes for public telephones, with a galvanized steel wire installed in each conduit. The one of the following reasons for providing this wire which is MOST acceptable is to

    A.   ensure that the conduit is clear
    B.   permit pulling in of wire at a later date
    C.   ground the system
    D.   limit corrosion of the interior surfaces of the conduit

12. An interior auxiliary fire alarm system to be installed in a building is to be of the coded city connected shunt-trip type. The one of the following which BEST describes the operation of this system is operating any station

    A.   sounds a coded signal on all bells and uses local power to trip a city box
    B.   operates the city box only
    C.   trips a city box using municipal system power and simultaneously sounds a coded signal on interior bells
    D.   operates interior gongs only

13. A magnetic motor starter is to be controlled with momentary start-stop pushbuttons at two locations. The number of control wires required, respectively, in the conduit between the controller and the first station and in the conduit between the two stations is

    A. 3 and 3   B. 4 and 4
    C. 3 and 4   D. 2 and 4

14. If the voltage on a 3-phase squirrel cage induction motor is reduced to 90% of its rating, the starting current

    A.   increases slightly   B.   is unchanged
    C.   decreases 10%   D.   decreases 20%

15. If the voltage on a 3-phase squirrel cage induction motor is reduced to 90% of its rating, the full load current   15._____

    A. decreases slightly   B. is unchanged
    C. increases 10%   D. increases 20%

16. A 3-conductor cable is used to provide a "hot" leg, switch leg and neutral between two outlets. The individual conductors are MOST commonly connected as follows: red is   16._____

    A. hot, white is neutral, black is switch
    B. switch, white is hot, black is neutral
    C. neutral, white is switch, black is hot
    D. switch, white is neutral, black is hot

17. To obtain a.c. current from a d.c. source of supply, it is BEST to use a(n)   17._____

    A. inverter   B. diode
    C. rectifier   D. shunt generator

18. Insulation resistance is commonly measured by means of a(n)   18._____

    A. ammeter   B. varmeter
    C. capacitance bridge   D. megger

19. A specification requires the installation of five pole, four wire, grounded 250 volt, 15 amp receptacles for 120/208 volt 3 ϕ 4 wire service, with matching plug and 15 foot #14AWG portable heavy duty cord. The number of conductors which the required cord MUST have is   19._____

    A. 3   B. 4
    C. 5   D. not clearly specified

Questions 20-21.

DIRECTIONS: The following questions 20 and 21 are to be answered in accordance with the information given below.

To get equivalent delta from wye

$$A = \frac{ab + bc + ac}{a}$$

$$B = \frac{ab + bx + ac}{b}$$

$$C = \frac{ab + bx + ac}{c}$$

To get equivalent wye from delta

$$a = \frac{BC}{A + B + C}$$

$$b = \frac{AC}{A + B + C}$$

$$c = \frac{AB}{A + B + C}$$

NOTE: The above formula indicates the relationship between equivalent wye and delta net works.

20. If, in a delta, the branches are resistors such that A=5 ohms, B=10 ohms, and C=10 ohms, the resistor of branch "a" of the equivalent wye is _____ ohms.

   A. 5   B. 10   C. 2   D. 4

21. In the problem 20 above, the resistor of branch "b" of the equivalent wye is _____ ohms.

   A. 10   B. 4   C. 2   D. 5

Questions 22-23.

DIRECTIONS: The following questions 22 and 23 should be answered in accordance with the paragraph below.

   Insulation resistance tests are best made with a direct-reading Megger. These tests can also be made with a high-resistance voltmeter and a source of d.c. supply. Assume that a direct reading instrument is not available but you have on hand a 100-volt voltmeter having a sensitivity of 5000 ohms per volt and a 100-volt battery. The battery is connected in series with the voltmeter. One free battery lead is connected to the wire whose insulation resistance is to be measured, and the other free lead to the grounded circuit. With this hookup, the voltmeter reads 50 volts.

22. The insulation resistance, in ohms, of the above conductor is

   A. 500   B. 5,000   C. 250,000   D. 500,000

23. The resistance, in ohms, of the above-mentioned voltmeter is

   A. 500   B. 5,000   C. 250,000   D. 500,000

24. An ammeter and voltmeter are connected through instrument transformers to measure the KVA of a balanced three phase load connected to a 2400 volt, 3-phase, 3 wire system. The PT is rated 2400/120 volts, and the CT is rated 200/5 amperes.
   If the ammeter reads 4 amps and the voltmeter 100 volts, the load, in KVA, is APPROXIMATELY

   A. 0.4   B. 6.8   C. 320   D. 555

25. A note on a lighting plan states: "All fluorescent fixtures shall be symmetrically spaced and oriented so that the major axis of the fixture is parallel to the major axis of the room." For a room 20' long by 16' wide, with four-four foot fixtures, the desired arrangement is: Fixtures parallel with and centered

   A. 4' from 20' wall, 5' from 16' wall
   B. 5' from 20' wall, 4' from 16' wall
   C. 4' from 16' wall, 5' from 20' wall
   D. 5' from 16' wall, 4' from 20' wall

Questions 26-31.

DIRECTIONS: The following questions 26 to 31 inclusive are to be answered in accordance with the provisions of the electrical code.

26. Individual conductors of multi-conductor control cables shall be   26.____

     A. color coded   B. clearly tagged at each end
     C. identified by painting   D. stranded

27. Terminals of motor-starting rheostats shall be   27.____

     A. suitable for solderless external connections only
     B. clearly marked to indicate wire to which they are to be connected
     C. equipped with barriers
     D. brought out to a suitable terminal block

28. Incandescent lamps can be used for control resistors   28.____

     A. under no circumstances
     B. as protective resistances provided they do not carry the main current
     C. for loads less than 1000 watts
     D. if mounted in porcelain receptacles

29. Wiring in battery rooms shall   29.____

     A. utilize lead covered cable
     B. be installed in rigid steel conduit
     C. be installed in Greenfield
     D. be enclosed in non-corrodible conduit or be exposed

30. Control switches for emergency lights in a theater shall be located   30.____

     A. where convenient to operating personnel
     B. in the lobby where accessible to authorized persons
     C. on the stage switchboard
     D. in the projection booth

31. Signal wires of sizes #18 or #16 shall be considered as properly protected by fuses rated   31.____
at _____ amps.

     A. 15   B. 20   C. 25   D. 30

32. If the voltage of a 3-phase squirrel cage induction motor is reduced to 90% of its rating,   32.____
the power factor

     A. increases slightly   B. is unchanged
     C. decreases slightly   D. decreases 10 points

33. To reverse the direction of rotation of a wound rotor 3-phase induction motor, interchange   33.____

     A. all line wires   B. all rotor connections
     C. any 2 rotor connections   D. any 2-line wires

Questions 34-36.

DIRECTIONS: The following questions 34 to 36 inclusive relate to the diagram appearing on the following page.

LEGEND

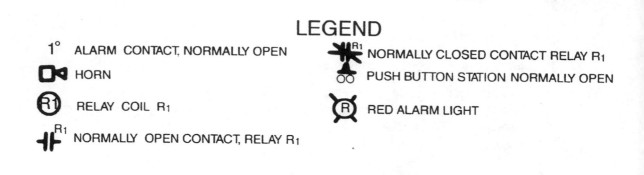

1°   ALARM CONTACT, NORMALLY OPEN

HORN

(R1) RELAY COIL R₁

NORMALLY OPEN CONTACT, RELAY R₁

NORMALLY CLOSED CONTACT RELAY R₁

PUSH BUTTON STATION NORMALLY OPEN

RED ALARM LIGHT

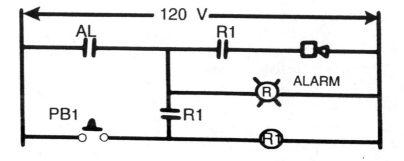

NOTE: The above diagram represents a simple alarm panel. Note that closing of the alarm contact causes the horn to sound and alarm lamp to light.

34. Assume that the alarm contact has closed. Then, pressing the PB

    A. causes the red alarm light to go out only as long as the button is depressed
    B. causes the horn to be silenced until the alarm contact opens and closes again
    C. tests the alarm light
    D. tests the alarm horn

35. The alarm light is illuminated

    A. only when the pushbutton is depressed
    B. only after the horn is silenced
    C. as long as the alarm contact is closed
    D. continuously

36. The relay R₁ has the following contacts:

    A. 2 N.O.   B. 2 N.C.
    C. 1 N.O. and 1N.C.   D. 2 N.O. and 1 N.C.

37. A blind hickey is used

    A. to cap a spare conduit
    B. in lieu of a fixture stud
    C. in lieu of a fixture extension
    D. to hang a lighting fixture on a gas outlet

Questions 38-41.

DIRECTIONS: The following questions 38 to 41 inclusive are to be answered in accordance
with the diagram below.

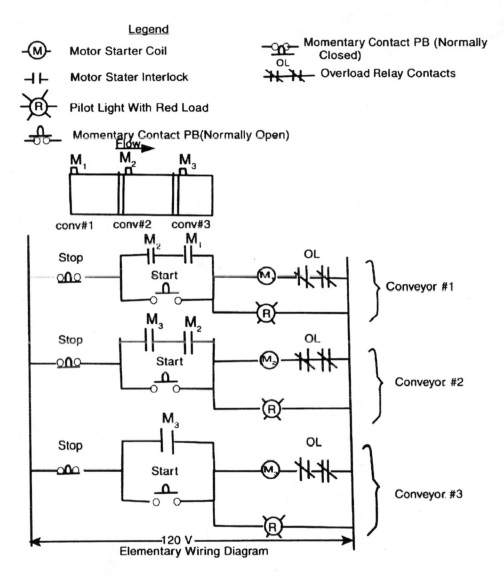

38.   For continuous operation of all conveyors,   38._____

    A.   conveyor #1 must be started first
    B.   conveyor #2 must be started first
    C.   conveyor #3 must be started first
    D.   conveyors can be started in any order

39.   Stopping of conveyor #3 will   39._____

    A.   not affect other conveyors
    B.   stop conveyor #2
    C.   stop conveyor #1
    D.   stop conveyors #1 and #2

40. Momentarily depressing the start PB of conveyor #2 before starting conveyor #3 or #1 will

    A. start conveyors #1 and #2
    B. start conveyor #2 and permit it to run continuously
    C. start conveyor #2 for only the time the button is depressed
    D. have no effect

41. When the thermal overload relays of conveyor #2 open,

    A. motor #2 only stops
    B. motors #1 and #2 will stop
    C. motor #1, #2, and #3 will stop
    D. an alarm will sound

42. An Erickson coupling is used

    A. to join sections of EMT
    B. to connect EMT to flexible conduit
    C. to connect two sections of rigid conduit when one section cannot be turned
    D. as a substitute for all thread

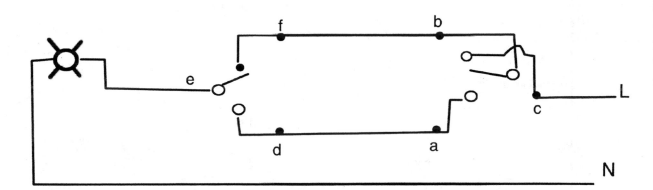

43. A light is to be controlled from two locations. It is connected with two 3-way switches as shown above and does not work properly.
To correct the wiring, the following changes should be made: Interchange connections

    A. e and f   B. b and c   C. a and b   D. a and c

44. Proper and economical control of lighting fixtures from three locations without the use of relays

    A. cannot be done
    B. requires a 3-way switch at each location
    C. requires two 3-way switches and one 4-way switch
    D. requires two 4-way switches and one 3-way switch

45. The outside diameter of a certain rigid steel conduit is measured to be approximately 2" (to the nearest 1/8 inch). The NOMINAL trade size is

    A. 2"   B. 1 1/2"   C. 1 1/4"   D. 2 1/2"

46. Electrical equipment can be secured to concrete walls by means of   46._____

    A. toggle bolts   B. wooden plugs and screws
    C. cut nails   D. lead shields

47. Continuity of an electrical circuit can conveniently be determined in the field by means of   47._____
a(n)

    A. smoke test   B. bell and battery set
    C. ammeter   D. Wheatstone Bridge

48. The speed of a motor can be measured by means of a   48._____

    A. potentiometer   B. megger
    C. tachometer   D. thermocouple

49. A test for transformer polarity is made on a
transformer rated 2400-240 volts by applying a voltage $V_1=120$ volts to the high voltage terminals H_1 and H_2 and measuring
the voltage between terminals H_2 and X_2.
(See diagram to the right.) If the transformer is of subtractive polarity, the voltmeter will read APPROXIMATELY _____
volts.   49._____

    A. 132   B. 12   C. 108   D. 0

50. An ammeter connected to the secondary of an energized metering transformer requires   50._____
repairs.
Before disconnecting the instrument, the electrician should

    A. open the secondary circuit
    B. short circuit the transformer secondary terminals
    C. short circuit the transformer primary terminals
    D. remove the transformer secondary fuses

KEY (CORRECT ANSWERS)

1. C	11. B	21. C	31. A	41. B
2. B	12. C	22. D	32. A	42. C
3. C	13. C	23. D	33. D	43. B
4. A	14. C	24. D	34. B	44. C
5. B	15. C	25. A	35. C	45. B
6. B	16. D	26. A	36. C	46. D
7. D	17. A	27. B	37. D	47. B
8. B	18. D	28. B	38. C	48. C
9. C	19. C	29. D	39. D	49. C
10. C	20. D	30. B	40. C	50. B

EXAMINATION SECTION
TEST 1

DIRECTIONS: Each question or incomplete statement is followed by several suggested answers or completions. Select the one that BEST answers the question or completes the statement. *PRINT THE LETTER OF THE CORRECT ANSWER IN THE SPACE AT THE RIGHT.*

1. The PRIMARY purpose of oil in an oil circuit breaker is to   1._____

    A. quench the arc
    B. lubricate the contacts
    C. reduce the reluctance of the core
    D. lubricate between the windings and the case

2. Assume that an auto transformer has a ratio of 2 to 1. With a primary voltage of 100 volts, 60 cycles, a.c., and a secondary load of 5 ohms, the current in the load is *most nearly*   2._____

    A. 20   B. 15   C. 10   D. 5

3. Assume that an auto transformer has a ratio of 2 to 1, with a primary voltage of 100 volts, 60 cycles, a.c., and a load of 5 ohms placed across the secondary.
Under the above conditions, the current in the secondary coil of the auto transformer is *most nearly*   3._____

    A. 20   B. 15   C. 10   D. 5

4. In fire extinguishers used to fight electrical fires, the chemical used as the fire extinguishing agent is   4._____

    A. H_2O B. KH_2 C. CO_2 D. CO

5. At a frequency of 60 cycles, the reactance in ohms of a condenser having a capacitance of 10 microfarads is *most nearly*   5._____

    A. 26.6   B. 37.7   C. 266   D. 377

6. Transformation of 3-phase to 2-phase systems can be obtained by using two special transformers. The COMMON method used for connecting these transformers is called a(n)   6._____

    A. open delta   B. zig-zag
    C. differential y on z   D. Scott or T

7. The electrolyte for a lead acid storage battery is properly prepared by pouring the   7._____

    A. sulphuric acid into the water
    B. water into the sulphuric acid
    C. potassium hydroxide into the water
    D. water into the potassium hydroxide

8.   The full-wave rectifier has a ripple frequency that is

A.   one-half that of the half-wave rectifier
B.   double that of the half-wave rectifier
C.   four times that of the half-wave rectifier
D.   equal to that of the half-wave rectifier

9.   Of the following, the one type of resistance wire which has an extremely low temperature co-efficient of resistance is known as

A.   Replevin   B.   Ribbon   C.   Maganin   D.   Bifilar

10.   In an a.c. dynamometer-type voltmeter, the deflections depend upon the square of the voltage. It can CORRECTLY be said that this instrument reads _____ values.

A.   average   B.   peak   C.   effective   D.   maximum

11.   The Dobrowolsky method used for three-wire generator systems is a very efficient means of obtaining a(n)

A.   neutral
C.   two-phase system

B.   V or open delta
D.   three-phase system

12.   Direct current armatures, wound with coils having fractional-pitch windings, have

A.   a coil span which is less than the pole pitch
B.   a coil span which is greater than the pole pitch
C.   more than 4 poles
D.   less than 4 poles

13.   To measure the current in a conductor without breaking into the conductor, you would use a(n)

A.   ampback
C.   ampule

B.   amprobe
D.   ampclip

14.   If two identical coils, each having an inductance of one henry, are connected in series aiding, the combined inductance, in henries, is

A.   exactly two
C.   exactly one

B.   greater than two
D.   less than one

15.   In a simplex lap winding, there are as many paths through the armature as there are

A.   armature slots
C.   commutator segments

B.   poles
D.   armature coils

16.   In a wave winding, the MINIMUM number of commutator brushes required is

A.   four
B.   two
C.   dependent on the number of commutator segments
D.   dependent on the armature coils

17. Some electricians have the faculty of knowing when there is work to be done and do not   17._____
have to be prompted to do it.
These electricians may be said to have

    A. initiative   B. individuality   C. virtue   D. discrimination

18. The number of threads per inch on a 1/4" diameter screw having American Standard   18._____
coarse threads is *most nearly*

    A. 20   B. 18   C. 14   D. 13

19. For general field or shop work, the proper tap drill size to use for a 6/32 machine screw is   19._____
most nearly number

    A. 50   B. 40   C. 36   D. 21

20. Graphical electrical symbols used on architectural plans are those recommended by the   20._____
A.S.A. The abbreviation A.S.A. refers to the

    A. American Society of Architects   B. American Standards Association
    C. Architectural Standards Association   D. Architectural Standards of America

21. Of the following, the BEST course of action to take if a motor bearing runs dangerously   21._____
hot Is to

    A. cool it quickly with cold water then rapidly decrease motor speed and oil the bear-
        ing freely
    B. oil the bearing freely and increase speed of motor
    C. decrease speed of motor until bearing cools sufficiently then stop the water and
        check for oil level and any damage to bearing
    D. add #40 SAE oil before increasing the load

22. Ten graduations on the barrel of a micrometer indicates an opening, in inches, of *most*   22._____
nearly

    A. 0.010   B. 0.050   C. 0.250   D. 0.270

23. The type of motor that may be designed to run on both a.c. or d.c. is the _____ motor.   23._____

    A. shunt   B. repulsion   C. compound   D. series

24. Assume that the cost of a certain wiring installation is broken down as follows: Materials   24._____
$1,200, Labor $800, and Rental of equipment $400. The percentage of the total cost of
the job that can be charged to Labor is *most nearly*

    A. 12.3   B. 33.3   C. 40.0   D. 66.6

25. Assume that it takes 4 electrician's helpers 6 days to do a certain job. Working at the   25._____
same rate of speed, the number of days it will take 3 electrician's helpers to do the same
job is

    A. 6   B. 7   C. 8   D. 9

26. Assume that a 120-volt, 25-cycle magnetic coil is to be rewound to operate properly on   26._____
60-cycles at the same voltage. If the coil at 25-cycles has 1,000 turns, at 60-cycles the
number of turns should be *most nearly*

    A. 2,400   B. 1,200   C. 416   D. 208

27. A coil having 50 turns of #14 wire as compared with a coil of the same diameter but having only 25 turns of #14 wire has

    A. a smaller inductance   B. a larger inductance
    C. the same inductance   D. the same impedance

Questions 28-40.

DIRECTIONS: The following questions 28 to 40 inclusive are to be answered in accordance with the requirements of the electrical code.
NOTE: Questions are to be answered assuming normal procedures, as given in the code. Do NOT use exceptions which are granted by special permission.

28. For elevator control wiring, conductors of 1/64 insulation may be used. The number of such conductors that may be installed in a conduit should be such that the sum of the cross-sectional area of all the conductors expressed as a percentage of the interior cross-sectional area of the conduit should NOT exceed

    A. 20%   B. 30%   C. 40%   D. 60%

29. Assume that the internal diameter of a two-inch conduit is 2.067 inches. The interior cross-sectional area, in square inches, of this conduit is *most nearly*

    A. 3.36   B. 4.79   C. 7.38   D. 9.90

30. No. 2 type R conductors in vertical raceways must be supported at intervals NOT greater than _____ feet.

    A. 50   B. 60   C. 80   D. 100

31. A unit of an electrical system, other than a conductor, which is intended to carry but NOT consume electrical energy is called a(n)

    A. device   B. circuit
    C. appliance   D. equipment

32. Three #4 A.W.G. rubber-covered, type R, conductors require a conduit having a diameter, in inches, of NOT less than

    A. 1/2   B. 3/4   C. 1   D. 1 1/4

33. For control conductors between motors and controllers, the MAXIMUM number of #10 type R conductors that may be put into a 1 1/4" conduit or tubing is

    A. 10   B. 13   C. 15   D. 17

34. The type of wire COMMONLY used for switchboard wiring is classified by type letter or letters

    A. TF   B. CF   C. TA   D. R

35. Wires in conduit (approved as to insulation and location) are required to have stranded conductors if they are

    A. No. 8 or larger   B. No. 6 or larger
    C. No. 6 or smaller   D. No. 8 or smaller

36. Bends of rigid conduit should be so made that the conduit will not be injured. Where rub-   36._____
ber conductors are used, the radius of the curve of the inner edge of any field bend
should be NOT less than _____ times the internal diameter of the conduit.

    A. 15   B. 10   C. 6   D. 4

37. In Class I hazardous locations, when a conduit leads from a hazardous location to a non-   37._____
hazardous location, the conduit should be sealed off with a sealing compound which is
NOT affected by the surrounding atmosphere and has a melting point of NOT less than

    A. 200°F   B. 150°F   C. 100°F   D. 75°F

38. Feeders should be of such size that the voltage drop up to the final distribution point   38._____
should NOT exceed

    A. 6%   B. 4 1/2%   C. 3%   D. 2 1/2%

39. For NOT more than three conductors in raceway (based on room temperature of 30°C or   39._____
86°F), the current carrying capacity in amperes of #10 type R insulated aluminum conductor is

    A. 10   B. 15   C. 25   D. 35

40. The MAXIMUM number of No. 12 wires terminating in a 1 1/2" x 3 1/4" octagonal junction   40._____
box should be

    A. 20   B. 15   C. 10   D. 5

KEY (CORRECT ANSWERS)

1.	A	11.	A	21.	C	31.	A
2.	C	12.	A	22.	C	32.	D
3.	D	13.	B	23.	D	33.	B
4.	C	14.	B	24.	B	34.	C
5.	C	15.	B	25.	C	35.	B
6.	D	16.	B	26.	C	36.	C
7.	A	17.	A	27.	B	37.	A
8.	B	18.	A	28.	C	38.	D
9.	C	19.	C	29.	A	39.	C
10.	C	20.	B	30.	D	40.	D

TEST 2

DIRECTIONS: Each question or incomplete statement is followed by several suggested answers or completions. Select the one that BEST answers the question or completes the statement. *PRINT THE LETTER OF THE CORRECT ANSWER IN THE SPACE AT THE RIGHT.*

1. Two copper conductors have the same length but the cross-section of one is twice that of the other. If the resistance of the one having a cross-section of twice the other is 10 ohms, the resistance of the other conductor, in ohms, is

   A. 5   B. 10   C. 20   D. 30

2. Assuming that copper weighs 0.32 lbs. per cubic inch, the weight, in lbs., of a bus bar 10' long and having a cross-section 2" x 1/2" is

   A. 120   B. 32   C. 3.2   D. 38.4

3. In a two-phase, three-wire system, the voltage between the common wire and either of the other two wires is 200 volts. The voltage between these other two wires is then *approximately* _____ volts.

   A. 200   B. 283   C. 141   D. 100

4. Three 30-ohm resistances are connected in delta across a 208-volt, 3-phase circuit. The line current, in amperes, is *approximately*

   A. 6.93   B. 13.86   C. 120   D. 12

5. A storage battery consists of three lead cells connected in series. On open circuit, the emf of the battery is 6.4 volts. When it delivers a current of 80 amperes, its terminal voltage drops to 4.80 volts. Its internal resistance, in ohms, is *approximately*

   A. 0.01   B. 0.02   C. 0.03   D. 0.04

6. In reference to question 5 above, the terminal voltage, in volts, when the battery delivers 50 amperes is *approximately*

   A. 5.9   B. 5.4   C. 4.9   D. 4.4

7. In order to magnetize a steel bar, a magnetomotive force of 1000 ampere turns is necessary. The voltage that MUST be applied to a coil of 100 turns and 10 ohms resistance is

   A. 1   B. 10   C. 100   D. 1000

8. Rosin is preferable to acid as a flux for soldering wire because rosin is

   A. a nonconductor   B. a dry powder
   C. a better conductor   D. noncorrosive

9. If, in tracing through an armature winding, all of the conductors are encountered before coming back to the starting point, there is but one closure and the winding is _____ reentrant.

   A. doubly   B. singly   C. triply   D. quintuply

10. A power factor meter is connected to a single-phase 2-wire circuit by means of _____ wires.   10._____

    A. 2   B. 3   C. 6   D. 5

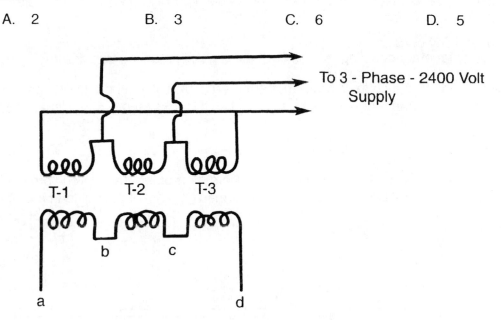

11. The above figure represents a transformer bank composed of 3 single-phase transformers each having a ratio of transformation equal to 20/1. The primary is already connected to the voltage supply, as shown in the diagram, while the secondary side is only "partly connected".   11._____
It is desired to connect the secondary of this transformer bank in delta. Before connecting a to d, the combination of voltages should correspond to one of the following:

    A.   Vab = 120, Vbc = 120, Vcd = 120 and Vad = 0
    B.   Vab = 120, Vbc = 120, Vcd = 120 and Vad = 120
    C.   Vab = 120, Vbc = 120, Vcd = 120 and Vad = 208
    D.   Vab = 208, Vbc = 208, Vcd = 208 and Vad = 0

12. With reference to question 11 above, assuming that the combination of voltages read as follows: Vab = 120 volts, Vbc = 120 volts, Vcd = 120 volts, Vad = 240 volts, and Vbd = 208 volts, before connecting a to d for a delta connection,   12._____

    A.   do nothing as the transformer bank is already phased out
    B.   secondary winding of T-1 should be reversed by interchanging its leads
    C.   secondary winding of T-2 should be reversed by interchanging its leads
    D.   secondary winding of T-3 should be reversed by changing its leads

13. The torque of a shunt motor varies as the   13._____

    A.   armature current   B.   square of the armature current
    C.   cube of the armature current   D.   cube of the field current

14. The armature of a synchronous converter has   14._____

    A.   3 slip rings for the ac and 2 slip rings for the dc
    B.   4 slip rings, 2 for the ac and 2 for the dc
    C.   a commutator and slip rings
    D.   no slip rings

15. An electrical device that transmits rotation from a driving to a driven member without mechanical contact – with stepless adjustable control and with almost instantaneous response – is the

    A. eddy current coupling
    C. planetary coupling

    B. universal coupling
    D. coupling transformer

16. According to the code, in order that armored cable will not be injured, the radius of the curve of the inner edge of any bend must be NOT less than _____ times the diameter of the cable.

    A. 3   B. 5   C. 7   D. 10

17. In accordance with the code, circuit breakers for motor branch circuit protection shall have continuous current ratings NOT less than _____ of the full load current of the motor.

    A. 110%   B. 115%   C. 120%   D. 125%

Meter resistance 5 Ω
Current for Full Scale deflection .01 amp

18. The above diagram represents the circuit of a multi-range ammeter. X-X is connected in series with an electric circuit for the purpose of measuring the current in that circuit. When slider S is connected to point B, the current I, in amperes, that will cause the meter to read full scale is *approximately*

    A. 30   B. 20   C. 10   D. 1

19. In reference to question 18 above, when slider S is connected to point C, the current I, in amperes, that will cause the meter to read full scale is *approximately*

    A. 30   B. 20   C. 10   D. 1

20. The code states that feeders over 40' in length supplying two branch circuits shall be NOT smaller than

    A. 2 No. 14 AWG
    C. 2 No. 10 AWG

    B. 2 No. 12 AWG
    D. 2 No. 8 AWG

21. Speed control by a method that requires two wound rotor induction motors with their rotors rigidly connected together is called speed control by

    A. change of poles   B. field control
    C. concatenation   D. voltage control

21.____

22. Before connecting an alternator to the bus bars and in parallel with other alternators, it is necessary that its voltage and frequency be the same as that of the bus bars but that

    A. the rotor revolve at synchronous speed
    B. the voltage be in phase opposition as well
    C. its power factor be not less than unit
    D. its power factor be greater than unit

22.____

23. A leather belt is used to drive a 3 kw dc generator by a 5 hp 3-phase induction motor. Adjustments for proper belt tension, with the generator running at full load, can be made with the aid of a

    A. 50-lb. weight as wide as the belt
    B. voltmeter and an ammeter
    C. power factor meter
    D. 3-phase wattmeter

23.____

24. The cold resistance of a 120-volt 100 watt Tungsten incandescent lamp is

    A. greater than its hot resistance
    B. smaller than the hot resistance
    C. approximately 100 ohms.
    D. equal to the hot resistance

24.____

25. The CORRECT value of the resistance of a field coil can be measured by using a(n)

    A. Schering bridge   B. ammeter and a voltmeter
    C. Kelvin double bridge   D. Maxwell bridge

25.____

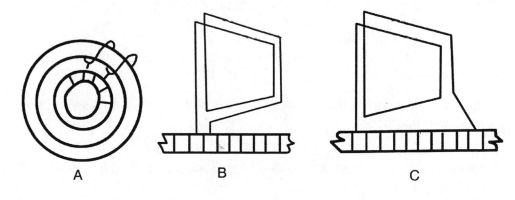

A   B   C

26. The three windings shown above belong, respectively, to the ring, lap, and wave types of _____ windings.

    A. closed-coil   B. open-coil
    C. reverse-coil   D. cumulative-coil

26.____

27. Simplex lap windings have as many armature circuits as there are   27

    A. commutator bars
    B. number of coils
    C. number of active conductors
    D. poles

28. The power factor of a single phase alternating current moter may be found by using one   28
of the following sets of ac instruments: one

    A. voltmeter and one phase-rotation meter
    B. voltmeter and one ammeter
    C. voltmeter, one ammeter, and one wattmeter
    D. voltmeter, one ammeter, and one watt-hour meter

29. When connecting wattmeters to ac moter circuits consuming large amounts of current, it   29
is necessary to use

    A. current transformers   B. potential transformers
    C. power shunts   D. isolation transformers

30. To control a lamp independently from five different points, you would use   30

    A. two 3-way and three 4-way switches
    B. four 3-way switches and one 4-way switch
    C. three 3-way and two 4-way switches
    D. three 4-way and two S.P.S.T. switches

31. The average life of a 100 watt incandescent light bulb is APPROXIMATELY _____   31
hours.

    A. 100   B. 400   C. 1000   D. 10,000

32. The efficiency in lumens per watt of a 40 watt fluorescent lamp   32

    A. is less than that of a 40 watt incandescent lamp
    B. is the same as that of a 40 watt incandescent lamp
    C. is greater than that of a 40 watt incandescent lamp
    D. may be greater or less than that of a 40 watt incandescent lamp, depending on the
        manufacturer

33. In order to use fluorescent lighting in a building which has only a 110 volt dc supply, it is   33
necessary to use fluorescent

    A. lamps designed for dc
    B. fixtures with an approved dc auxiliary or inductance unit and a series resistance of
        the correct value
    C. fixtures ordinarily used on ac
    D. fixtures ordinarily used on ac but equipped with a rectifier

34. Electrical contacts are opened or closed when the electrical current energizes the coils   34
of a device called a

    A. reactor   B. transtat
    C. relay   D. thermostat

35. Transformer cores are composed of laminated sheet steel in order to keep the _____ loss to a minimum.

    35.____

    A. hysteresis
    C. eddy current
    B. windage
    D. copper

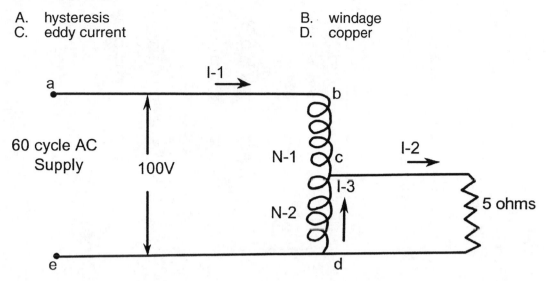

36. An auto transformer whose primary is bd is connected across a 100-volt ac supply as shown in the above diagram. The load of 5 ohms is connected across points c and d. If it is assumed that N-1 = N-2 (that is, point c is the midpoint of the winding), current I-1, in amperes, is *approximately* equal to

    36.____

    A. 5   B. 10   C. 15   D. 20

37. In reference to question 36 above, current I-2, in amperes, is *approximately* equal to

    37.____

    A. 5   B. 10   C. 15   D. 20

38. In reference to question 36 above, current I-3, in amperes, is *approximately* equal to

    38.____

    A. 5   B. 10   C. 15   D. 20

39. The transformer is based on the principle that energy may be effectively transferred by induction from one set of coils to another by a varying magnetic flux, provided both sets of coils

    39.____

    A. are not a common magnetic circuit
    B. have the same number of turns
    C. are on a common magnetic circuit
    D. do not have the same number of turns

40. In a transformer the induced emf per turn in the secondary winding is

    40.____

    A. equal to the induced emf per turn in the primary winding
    B. not equal to the induced emf per turn in the primary winding
    C. equal to the induced emf per turn in the primary winding multiplied by the ratio N-1/N-2
    D. equal to the induced emf per turn in the primary winding divided by the ratio N-1/N-2

KEY (CORRECT ANSWERS)

1.	C	11.	A	21.	C	31.	C
2.	D	12.	D	22.	B	32.	C
3.	B	13.	A	23.	D	33.	B
4.	D	14.	C	24.	B	34.	C
5.	B	15.	A	25.	B	35.	C
6.	B	16.	B	26.	A	36.	A
7.	C	17.	B	27.	D	37.	B
8.	D	18.	C	28.	C	38.	A
9.	B	19.	B	29.	A	39.	C
10.	B	20.	C	30.	A	40.	A

TEST 3

DIRECTIONS: Each question or incomplete statement is followed by several suggested answers or completions. Select the one that BEST answers the question or completes the statement. *PRINT THE LETTER OF THE CORRECT ANSWER IN THE SPACE AT THE RIGHT.*

1. Five 100-watt, 120-volt lamps connected in series across a 600-volt circuit will draw a current, in amperes, of *most nearly*   1.____

   A. 4.2   B. .8   C. .6   D. .4

2. For a given level of illumination in a certain lighting installation, the cost of electrical energy using fluorescent lighting fixtures as compared with incandescent lighting fixtures is   2.____

   A. more   B. less
   C. the same   D. dependent on the load

3. Assume that three 20.8 ohm resistances are connected in delta across a 208-volt, 3-phase circuit. The line current, in amperes, will be *most nearly*   3.____

   A. 20.8   B. 17.3   C. 10.4   D. 8.6

4. Assume that three 10-ohm resistances are connected in wye across a 208-volt, 3-phase circuit.
   The power, in watts, dissipated in this resistance load will be *most nearly*   4.____

   A. 4320   B. 1440   C. 2160   D. 720

5. A tungsten incandescent lamp has its GREATEST resistance when the lamp is   5.____

   A. cold
   B. burning at full brilliance
   C. burning at half brilliance
   D. burning at one-quarter brilliance

6. Direct current can be converted to alternating current by means of a(n)   6.____

   A. inverter   B. rectifier
   C. filter   D. selsyn

7. The direction of rotation of a d.c. shunt motor can be reversed by   7.____

   A. interchanging the line terminals
   B. reversing the field and armature current
   C. reversing the field or armature current
   D. reversing the current in any one of the commutating pole windings

8. The insulation resistance of the conductors of an electrical installation is measured or tested with a(n)   8.____

   A. strobe   B. ammeter   C. Q-meter   D. megger

9. In dealing with electrician's helpers, it is MOST important that the electrician be   9.____

   A. stern   B. fair   C. blunt   D. chummy

10. If an electrician does not understand the instructions that are given to him by his fore- 1
man, the BEST thing to do is to

    A. work out the solution to the problem himself
    B. do the job the way he thinks is best
    C. get one of the other electricians to do the job
    D. ask that the instructions be repeated and clarified

11. Assume that a group of dc. shunt motors is 500 ft. from a power panel and is supplied by 1
two 350,000 c.m. conductors with a maximum load for this circuit of 190 amps.
If the resistance of 1000 feet of 350,000 c.m. conductor is 0.036 ohm, and the voltage
at the power panel is 230 volts, the voltage at the load will be *most nearly*

    A. 217   B. 220   C. 223   D. 229

12. The power in a three-phase, three wire circuit is measured by means of the two-watt 1
meter method. When the reading of one wattmeter is exactly the same as the reading of
the other wattmeter, the power factor will be

    A. 1   B. .866   C. .5   D. 0

13. Assume that a fluorescent lamp blinks "on" and "off." 1
This may

    A. in time result in injury to the ballast
    B. cause a fuse to blow
    C. be due to a shorted switch
    D. be caused by an abnormally high voltage

14. The one of the following troubles which is NOT a cause of sparking at the commutator of 1
a dc. motor is

    A. a short-circuited armature coil
    B. an open-circuited armature coil
    C. vibration of the machine
    D. running below rated speed

15. The current, in amperes, of a 220-volt, 10-HP, d.c. motor having an efficiency of 90% is 1
approximately

    A. 37.6   B. 34   C. 28.6   D. 40.5

16. The grid-controlled gas-type electronic tube MOST often used in motor control circuits is 1
the

    A. ignitron   B. thyratron
    C. strobostron   D. magnetron

17. With reference to electronic control work, the vacuum tube element or electrode which is 1
placed in the electron stream and to which a control voltage may be applied is the

    A. plate   B. grid   C. filament   D. cathode

18. Full-wave rectifiers   18.____

    A.   may be built with one tungar bulb
    B.   produce a.c. current which contains some d.c.
    C.   are used to change dp. current to a.c.
    D.   must have at least two tungar bulbs

19. Assume that two batteries are connected in multiple. If the voltage and internal resis-   19.____
tance of one battery are 6 volts and 0.2 ohms, respectively, and the voltage and internal
resistance of the other battery are 3 volts and 0.1 ohms, respectively, the circulating current, in amperes, will be *approximately*

    A. 2   B. 5   C. 10   D. 30

20. In a single phase motor, the temporary production of a substitute for a two-phase current   20.____
so as to obtain a makeshift rotating field in starting is COMMONLY called

    A.   phase splitting   B.   phase spread
    C.   phase transformation   D.   phantom circuit

21. If a solenoid is grasped in the right hand so that the fingers point in the direction in which   21.____
the current is flowing in the wires, the thumb, extended, will point in the direction of the
_____ pole.

    A.   negative   B.   positive
    C.   south   D.   north

22. The junction of two dissimilar metals produces a flow of current when the junction is   22.____

    A.   wet
    B.   heated
    C.   highly polished
    D.   placed in a dp. magnetic field

23. The active material in the positive plates of a charged lead acid storage battery is   23.____

    A.   lead carbonate   B.   lead acetate
    C.   lead peroxide   D.   sponge lead

24. The negative plates of a charged lead acid storage battery are composed of   24.____

    A.   lead carbonate   B.   lead acetate
    C.   lead peroxide   D.   sponge lead

25. A constant horsepower two-speed squirrel cage induction motor may be made to run at   25.____
the higher speed by

    A.   changing the connections to make it an eight-pole motor
    B.   decreasing the rotor resistance
    C.   changing the connections so that the motor has the lesser number of poles
    D.   changing the connections so that the motor has the greater number of poles

26. A constant horsepower two-speed squirrel cage induction motor has its stator coils and   26.____
the line wires connected so as to form a series delta connection. Assume that the connections of the stator coils and the lines are now changed so as to form a parallel-wye
connection. Under these conditions, the motor will now have _____ poles and _____
speed.

A. fewer; higher
C. more; higher

B. fewer; lower
D. more; lower

27. Assume that a circuit carrying 8 amperes of d.c. current and 6 amperes of a.c. current is connected to a hot wire ammeter. The reading, in amperes, of this meter will be *most nearly*

    A. 16   B. 14   C. 12   D. 10

28. To start a 20 HP., 3-phase, 208 volt plain induction motor, it is good practice to use a

    A. compensator
    C. rotor box

    B. 3-point box
    D. 4-point box

29. A 25-ampere, 50 millivolt d.c. shunt has a resistance, in ohms, of *approximately*

    A. 0.002   B. 0.02   C. 0.5   D. 5.

30. When a relay coil is energized by applying the rated voltage across its terminals, a certain time, in seconds, must elapse from the moment the circuit is completed before the current attains approximately 2/3 of its full strength.
This elapsed time is

    A. entirely dependent on the coil resistance
    B. entirely dependent on the coil inductance
    C. proportional to the coil resistance divided by the coil inductance
    D. proportional to the coil inductance divided by the coil resistance

31. For proper operation all gas discharge lamps require

    A. a series resistor
    C. some sort of ballast

    B. a parallel resistor
    D. a starter.

32. To obtain proper short-circuit protection for a service, one should use a

    A. limiting resistor
    C. time delay relay

    B. time delay breaker
    D. current limiting fuse

33. A neon test lamp can be used by an electrician to test

    A. the phase rotation of a source of supply
    B. the power factor of a source of supply
    C. a source of supply to see if it is a.c. or d.c.
    D. the field intensity of a relay magnet

34. A d.c. milliammeter may be adapted for a.c. measurements by using with it a(n)

    A. paper condenser
    C. instrument transformer

    B. instrument shunt
    D. selenium rectifier

35. A static capacitor used for power factor correction is connected to the line in

    A. parallel with a machine drawing lagging current
    B. series with a machine drawing lagging current
    C. parallel with a machine drawing leading current
    D. series with a machine drawing leading current

36. To start a squirrel cage induction motor with an across-the-line starter, without undue dis-   36.____
turbance to the line voltage, the capacity of the motor in HP should NOT exceed

   A.   100   B.   75   C.   50   D.   5

37. The type of a.c. motor MOST commonly used where considerable starting torque is   37.____
required is the

   A.   squirrel cage induction motor
   B.   wound rotor induction motor
   C.   shunt motor
   D.   synchronous motor

38. On direct current controllers where it is necessary to remove or replace blow-out coils, it   38.____
is IMPORTANT to

   A.   see that the positive pole is facing down
   B.   see that the negative pole is facing up
   C.   insert the blow-out coils to give the proper polarity
   D.   cross the coil leads before connecting them

39. The size of the fuse to be used in a circuit depends upon the   39.____

   A.   connected load
   B.   size of wire
   C.   voltage of the line
   D.   size and rating of the switch

40. Assume that a d.c. contactor coil has two turns short-circuited. In operation, it will   40.____

   A.   burn out
   B.   hum excessively
   C.   continue to operate at reduced efficiency
   D.   vibrate due to the high induced current

_____

KEY (CORRECT ANSWERS)

1. B	11. C	21. D	31. C
2. B	12. A	22. B	32. D
3. B	13. A	23. C	33. C
4. A	14. D	24. D	34. D
5. B	15. A	25. C	35. A
6. A	16. B	26. D	36. D
7. C	17. B	27. D	37. B
8. D	18. D	28. A	38. C
9. B	19. C	29. A	39. B
10. D	20. A	30. D	40. C

_____

EXAMINATION SECTION
TEST 1

DIRECTIONS: Each question or incomplete statement is followed by several suggested answers or completions. Select the one that *BEST* answers the question or completes the statement. *PRINT THE LETTER OF THE CORRECT ANSWER IN THE SPACE AT THE RIGHT.*

1. That system of electric braking in which the traction motors are used as generators and the kinetic energy of the load is used as the actuating means for exerting a retarding force is known as _____ braking.   1._____

    A. track   B. magnetic   C. dynamic   D. generator

2. Thermal overload protective devices used for motor running protection protect the motor against   2._____

    A. a short-circuit   B. overcurrent at starting
    C. transient overloads   D. normal operating overloads

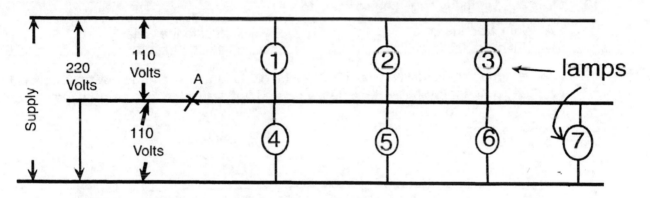

3. In the above diagram, the center conductor breaks at point A.   3._____

    A. Lamps 1, 2, and 3 will burn with greater brilliancy than lamps 4, 5, 6 and 7.
    B. Lamps 1, 2, and 3 will burn dimmer than lamps 4, 5, 6, and 7.
    C. All lamps will be extinguished.
    D. All lamps will burn with the same brilliancy that they had before the center lead opened.

4. In ordering standard cartridge fuses it is necessary to specify ONLY the   4._____

    A. current capacity
    B. voltage of the circuit
    C. current capacity and the voltage of the circuit
    D. power to be dissipated

5. The current input per phase under rated-load conditions for a 200-H.P., 3 phase, 2300-volt, 0.8 P. F., induction motor which is 90% efficient is _____ amperes.   5._____

    A. 52   B. 90   C. 41.6   D. 46.8

6. Referring to problem 5 above, the power input under rated-load conditions is APPROXI-MATELY   6._____

    A. 149 K.W.   B. 96 K.W.   C. 166 K.W.   D. 332 K.W.

7. Three single-phase transformers are connected in delta on both the primary and secondary sides.
If one of the transformers burns out the system can continue to operate but its capacity, in terms of the capacity of the original arrangement, is reduced to

    A. 66 2/3%   B. 57.8%   C. 115%   D. 100%

8. In order to successfully operate two compound-wound d.c. generators in parallel it is necessary to use

    A. a compensating winding   B. an equalizer connection
    C. a series field diverter   D. commutating poles

9. If a given machine requires a full-load torque of 30 pound-feet and runs at a speed of 1800 R.P.M., the size of direct-coupled motor required to drive this machine is APPROXIMATELY _____ H.P.

    A. 10.3   B. 20.6   C. 15.3   D. 5.2

10. Oil is used in many large transformers to

    A. lubricate the core   B. lubricate the coils
    C. insulate the coils   D. insulate the core

11. A certain machine is driven by a 1750-R.P.M. d.c. shunt motor. If the power supply is to be changed to three-phase, 60 cycles, a.c., the MOST suitable replacement motor would be a _____ motor.

    A. series   B. repulsion
    C. squirrel-cage induction   D. capacitor

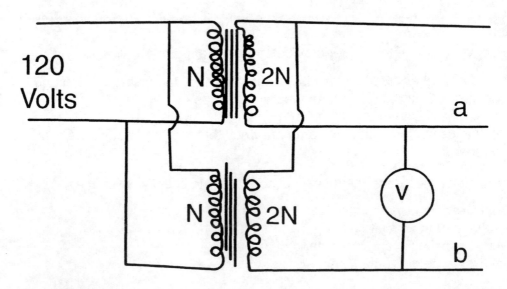

12. Two transformers with ratios of 1.2 are to be connected in parallel. To test for proper connections the circuit of the above diagram is used.
The transformers may be connected in parallel by connecting lead *a* to lead *b* if the voltmeter shown reads _____ volts.

    A. 120   B. 240   C. zero   D. 480

13. You were asked to calculate the electric bill for the last month. The kilowatt-hour meter reads 99,010 K.W.-hrs. at the end of the previous month and now reads 00,110 K.W.-hrs. The demand meter reads 75 K.W.

13.____

The energy rate is:

For the first 500 K.W.-hrs.	$0.04 per K.W.-hr.
For the next 300 K.W.-hrs.	$0.03 per K.W.-hr.
For the next 200 K.W.-hrs.	$0.02 per K.W.-hr.
For all in excess of 100 K.W.-hrs.	$0.01 per K.W.-hr.

The demand rate is $0.50 per K.W.
The total electric bill is

   A. $71.50   B. $67.50   C. $83.50   D. $74.50

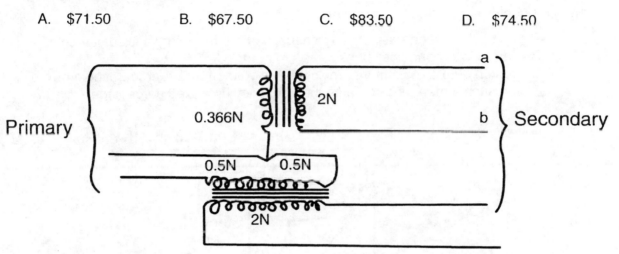

14. If the primary leads in the above diagram are connected to a three-phase, three-wire, 208 volt system and the transformation ratios are as indicated on the diagram, the secondary leads will form a _____ -phase, _____ -wire system.

14.____

A.	three	four
B.	two	four
C.	four	five
D.	three	three

15. In the circuit of the above diagram, the voltage between the secondary leads *a* and *b* is _____ volts.

15.____

   A. 208   B. 120   C. 416   D. 240

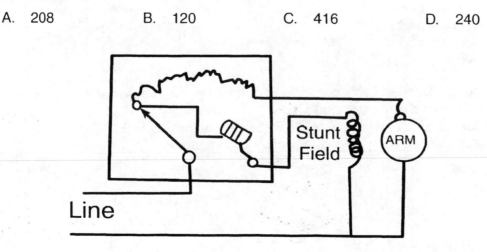

16. The circuit of the above diagram shows a d.c. motor starter.
One of the features of this starting box is a(n) _____ release.

    A. overload   B. no-field   C. reverse-current   D. underload

17. For starting a three-phase induction motor a three-phase transformer is used with its primaries connected in delta and its secondaries connected in delta for starting and in wye for running.
The ratio of the running to the starting voltage is

    A. 3 : 1   B. 2 : 1   C. 1.73 : 1   D. 1.41 : 1

18. A booster transformer is a transformer connected

    A. in such a manner as to increase the load on the line by a fixed percentage
    B. as a delta-connected bank
    C. as an auto-transformer to raise the line voltage by a fixed percentage
    D. in such a manner as to raise the frequency by a fixed percentage

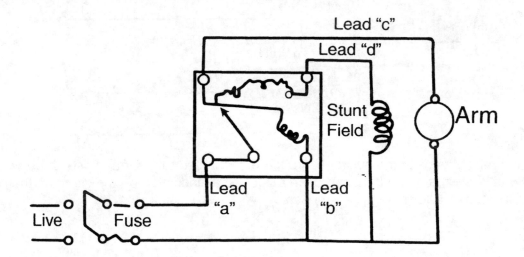

19. The motor shown in the above figure does not operate correctly. When the line switch is closed the fuses blow.
To correct this fault leads _____ and _____ should be interchanged.

    A. leads a and b
    B. leads a and c
    C. leads b and d
    D. leads c and d

20. A standard stranded cable contains 19 strands. When measured with a micrometer the diameter of each strand is found to be 105.5 mils.
If, under certain conditions, the allowable current density is 600 C.M. per ampere the allowable current-carrying capacity of this conductor is _____ amperes.

    A. 236   B. 176.3   C. 352.5   D. 705

21. For MAXIMUM safety the magnetic contactors used for reversing the direction of rotation of a motor should be   21.____

    A. electrically interlocked
    B. electrically and mechanically interlocked
    C. mechanically interlocked
    D. operated from independent sources

22. When the starter for a 250-volt, direct-current shunt motor whose full-load armature current is 20 amperes, is in the first contact postion, the total resistance in the armature circuit, to permit the motor to start with 150% of rated torque, should be APPROXIMATELY _____ ohms.   22.____

    A. 5   B. 8   C. 12   D. 20

23. If the allowable current density for copper bus bars is 1000 amperes per square inch, the current-carrying capacity of a circular copper bar having a diameter of two inches is APPROXIMATELY _____ amperes.   23.____

    A. 1050   B. 2320   C. 3140   D. 4260

24. A rotary converter, operating at unity power factor, may be made to take a loading power factor by   24.____

    A. *increasing* the d.c. field strength of the machine
    B. *decreasing* the d.c. field strength of the machine
    C. *decreasing* the speed at which it operates
    D. *increasing* the speed at which it operates

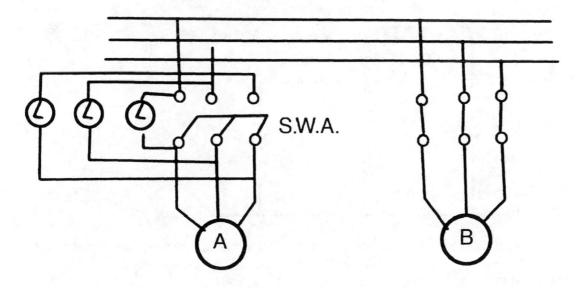

25. Two alternators are to be synchronized for parallel operation, the correct synchronization being indicated by three lamps, as shown in the above diagram.
The CORRECT time to close switch *A* is   25.____

    A. when the lamps are at maximum brilliancy
    B. when the lamps are dark
    C. just before the lamps reach maximum brilliancy
    D. just after the lamps reach maximum brilliancy

26. The maximum voltage-drop between a d.c. motor and switchboard is not to exceed one   2
    percent of the supply voltage.
    If the supply voltage is 200 volts, the full-load current of the motor 100 amperes, the
    distance from the switchboard to the motor 100 feet, and the resistivity of copper 10
    ohms per C.M.-foot, the size wire required in C.M. is

    A. 25,000   B. 50,000   C. 100,000   D. 200,000

27. One foot of a certain size of nichrome wire has a resistance of 1.63 ohms.   2
    To make a heating element for a toaster that will use 5 amperes at 110 volts, the num-
    ber of feet of wire needed is APPROXIMATELY

    A. 17.9   B. 8.2   C. 5.5   D. 13.5

28. A tri-free circuit breaker is one that   2

    A. is tripped from a shunt-circuit through a relay
    B. can be tripped only by an operator
    C. cannot be tripped when the operating lever is held in the closed position
    D. can be tripped by the overload mechanism even though the operating lever is held
        in the closed position

29. The following equipment is required for a 2-*line return-call* electric bell circuit: 2 bells, 2   2
    metallic lines,

    A. 2 ordinary push-buttons, and one set of batteries
    B. 2 return-call push-buttons and 2 sets of batteries
    C. 2 return-call push-buttons and one set of batteries
    D. one ordinary push-button, one return-call push button and one set of batteries

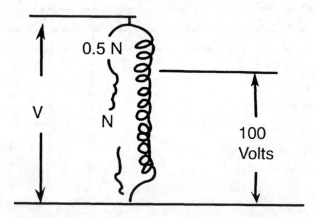

30. An auto-transformer with turns ratio as indicated in the above sketch is connected to a   3
    100-volt, 60-cycle supply on the low-tension side.
    The voltage, V, on the high tension side is _____ volts.

    A. 50   B. 100   C. 150   D. 200

31. The MINIMUM size of grounding conductor for a direct or alternating-current system is   3

    A. No. 14   B. No. 10   C. No. 8   D. No. 6

32. The thickness of insulation for a No. 8 rubber-covered conductor for use at NOT more than 2000 volts shall be _____ of an inch.

    A. 2/64ths   B. 3/64ths   C. 4/64ths   D. 5/64ths

32._____

33. A gutter whose width is 36 inches shall be constructed of sheet metal of thickness NOT less than No. _____ U.S. standard sheet metal gauge.

    A. 10   B. 12   C. 14   D. 16

33._____

34. The MAXIMUM voltage permitted on the push buttons of elevator signalling circuits shall be _____ volts to ground.

    A. 300   B. 125   C. 250   D. 600

34._____

35. Electric motors installed in hospital operating rooms shall be of the _____ proof type.

    A. water   B. explosion   C. dust   D. light

35._____

36. Connecting batteries in parallel instead of in series _____ of the batteries.

    A. *increases* the current output
    B. *decreases* the life
    C. *increases* the voltage
    D. *decreases* the current output

36._____

37. To charge a storage battery, one would use

    A. either a.c. or d.c.   B. a.c. only
    C. d.c. only   D. only low frequency a.c.

37._____

38. A transformer is USUALLY used to

    A. change a.c. to d.c.
    B. raise or lower a.c. voltage
    C. change d.c. to a.c.
    D. change the frequency of the a.c. supply

38._____

39. The commutator of a d.c. generator

    A. keeps the current flowing in one direction in the load circuit
    B. reverses the current direction in the armature
    C. acts only as a sliding electrical contact
    D. changes a.c. to d.c. within the armature

39._____

40. The number of fresh dry cells that should be connected in series to obtain 12 volts is

    A. 2   B. 6   C. 8   D. 12

40._____

KEY (CORRECT ANSWERS)

1.	C	11.	C	21.	B	31.	C
2.	D	12.	C	22.	B	32.	D
3.	A	13.	A	23.	C	33.	A
4.	C	14.	B	24.	A	34.	A
5.	A	15.	C	25.	B	35.	B
6.	C	16.	B	26.	C	36.	A
7.	B	17.	C	27.	D	37.	C
8.	B	18.	C	28.	D	38.	B
9.	A	19.	D	29.	B	39.	A
10.	C	20.	C	30.	C	40.	C

TEST 2

DIRECTIONS: Each question or incomplete statement is followed by several suggested answers or completions. Select the one that *BEST* answers the question or completes the statement. *PRINT THE LETTER OF THE CORRECT ANSWER IN THE SPACE AT THE RIGHT.*

1. Of the following, the BEST conductor of electricity is   1.____

   A. tungsten   B. iron   C. aluminum   D. carbon

2. A 600-volt cartridge fuse is MOST readily distinguished from a 250-volt cartridge fuse of   2.____
   the same ampere rating by comparing the

   A. insulating materials used   B. shape of the ends
   C. diameters   D. lengths

3. Many power-transformer cases are filled with oil.   3.____
   The purpose of the oil Is to

   A. prevent rusting of the core
   B. reduce a.c. hum
   C. insulate the coils from the case
   D. transmit heat from the coils and core

4. In order to make certain that a 600-volt circuit is dead before working on it, the BEST pro- 4.____
   cedure is to

   A. test with a voltmeter
   B. *short* the circuit quickly with a piece of insulated wire
   C. see if any of the insulated conductors are warm
   D. disconnect one of the wires of the circuit near the feed

5. When closing an exposed knife switch on a panel, the action should be positive and rapid   5.____
   because there is less likelihood of

   A. the operator receiving a shock
   B. the operator being burned
   C. the fuse blowing
   D. injury to equipment connected to the circuit

6. Lubrication is never used on   6.____

   A. a knife switch
   B. a die when threading conduit
   C. wires being pulled into a conduit
   D. a commutator

7. If one plug fuse in a 110-volt circuit blows because of a short-circuit, a 110-volt lamp   7.____
   screwed into the fuse socket will

   A. burn dimly   B. remain dark   C. burn out   D. burn normally

8. Of the following, the LEAST undesirable practice if a specified wire size is not available   8.____
   for part of a circuit is to

A. use two wires of 1/2 capacity in parallel as a substitute
B. use the next larger size wire
C. use a smaller size wire if the length is short
D. reduce the size of the fuse and use smaller wire

9. If it is necessary to increase slightly the tension of an ordinary coiled spring in a relay, the PROPER procedure is to

A. cut off one or two turns
B. compress it slightly
C. stretch it slightly
D. unhook one end, twist and replace

10. As compared with solid wire, stranded wire of the same gage size is

A. given a higher current rating
C. larger in total diameter
B. easier to skin
D. better for high voltage

11. Motor frames are USUALLY positively grounded by a special connection in order to

A. remove static
C. provide a neutral
B. protect against lightening
D. protect against shock

12. If a live conductor is contacted accidentally, the severity of the electrical shock is determined PRIMARILY by

A. the size of the conductor
B. whether the current is a.c. or d.c.
C. the contact resistance
D. the current in the conductor

13. If a snap switch rated at 5 amperes is used for an electric heater which draws 10 amperes, the MOST likely result is that the

A. circuit fuse will be blown
B. circuit wiring will become hot
C. heater output will be halved
D. switch contacts will become hot

14. To straighten a long length of wire which has been tightly coiled, before pulling it into a conduit run, a good method is to

A. roll the wire into a coil in the opposite direction
B. fasten one end to the floor and whip it against the floor from the other end
C. draw it over a convenient edge
D. hold the wire at one end and twist it with the pliers from the other end

15. The wire size MOST commonly used for branch circuits in residences is

A. #14   B. #16   C. #12   D. #18

16. If the applied voltage on an incandescent lamp is increased 10%, the lamp will

A. have a longer life
B. burn more brightly
C. consume less power
D. fail by insulation breakdown

17. You would expect that the overload trip coil on an ordinary air circuit breaker would have   17.____

    A. heavy wire   B. fine wire
    C. many turns   D. heavily insulated wire

18. A cycle counter is an electrical timer which, when energized by alternating current,   18.____
counts the number of cycles until it is de-energized.
If a cycle counter is energized from a 60-cycle power supply for ten seconds, the reading of the instrument should be

    A. 6   B. 10   C. 60   D. 600

19. The MOST practical way to determine in the field if a large coil of #14 wire has the   19.____
required length for a given job is to

    A. weigh the coil
    B. measure one turn and count the turns
    C. unroll it into another coil
    D. make a visual comparison with a full coil

20. A frequency meter is constructed as a potential device, that is, to be connected across   20.____
the line.
A logical reason for this is that

    A. only the line voltage has frequency
    B. a transformer may then be used with it
    C. the reading will be independent of the varying current
    D. it is safer than a series device

21. It is usually not safe to connect 110 volts d.c. to a magnet coil designed for 110 volts a.c.   21.____
because the

    A. insulation is insufficient   B. iron may overheat
    C. wire may overheat   D. inductance may be too high

22. The MOST satisfactory temporary replacement for a 40-watt, 120-volt incandescent   22.____
lamp, if an identical replacement is not available, is a lamp rated at _____ watts,
_____ volts.

    A. 100; 240   B. 60; 130   C. 40; 32   D. 15; 120

23. If the following bare copper wire sizes were arranged in the order of increasing weight   23.____
per 1000 feet, the CORRECT arrangement would be

    A. #00, #40, #8   B. #40, #00, #8
    C. #00, #8, #40   D. #40, #8, #00

24. The purpose of having a rheostat in the field circuit of a d.c. shunt motor is to   24.____

    A. control the speed of the motor
    B. minimize the starting current
    C. limit the field current to a safe value
    D. reduce sparking at the brushes

25. The resistance of a 1000-ft. length of a certain size copper wire is required to be 10.0 ohms ± 2%.
    This wire would NOT be acceptable if the resistance was _____ ohms.

    A. 10.12   B. 10.02   C. 10.22   D. 9.82

26. The LEAST important action in making a good soldered connection between two wires is to

    A. use the proper flux   B. clean the wires well
    C. use plenty of solder   D. use sufficient heat

27. Of the following, the BEST conductor of electricity is

    A. aluminum   B. carbon   C. copper   D. water

28. Good practice requires that the end of a piece of conduit be reamed after it has been cut to length.
    The purpose of the reaming is to

    A. prevent insulation damage when pulling in the wires
    B. finish the conduit accurately to length
    C. make the threading easier
    D. remove loose rust

29. According to the national electrical code, a run of conduit between two outlet boxes should not contain more than four quarter bends.
    The MOST likely reason for this limitation is that more bends will

    A. result in cracking the conduit
    B. make the pulling of the wire too difficult
    C. increase the wire length unnecessarily
    D. not be possible in one standard length of conduit

30. Asbestos is commonly used as the covering of electric wires in locations where there is likely to be high

    A. voltage   B. temperature   C. humidity   D. current

31. Portable lamp cord is LIKELY to have

    A. steel armor   B. stranded wires
    C. paper insulation   D. number 8 wire

32. The one of the following terms which could NOT correctly be used in describing a knife switch is

    A. quick-break   B. single throw   C. four-pole   D. toggle

33. With respect to common electric light bulbs, it is CORRECT to state that the

    A. circuit voltage has no effect on the life of the bulb
    B. filament is made of carbon
    C. base has a left hand thread
    D. lower wattage bulb has the higher resistance

34. The resistance of a 1000-foot coil of a certain size copper wire is 10 ohms. If 300 feet are cut off, the resistance of the remainder of the coil is _____ ohms.

    A. 7   B. 3   C. 0.7   D. 0.3

  34.____

35. The term *l5 ampere* is COMMONLY used in identifying a(n)

    A. insulator   B. fuse   C. conduit   D. outlet box

  35.____

36. When connecting the two lead wires of a test instrument to a live d.c. circuit, the BEST procedure is to first make the negative or ground connection and then the positive connection.
The reason for this procedure is that

    A. electricity flows from positive to negative
    B. there is less danger of accidental shock
    C. the reverse procedure may blow the fuse
    D. less arcing will occur when the connection is made

  36.____

37. To make a good soldered connection between two stranded wires, it is LEAST important to

    A. twist the wires together before soldering
    B. use enough heat to make the solder flow freely
    C. clean the wires carefully
    D. apply solder to each strand before twisting the two wires together

  37.____

38. When a step-up transformer is used, it increases the

    A. voltage   B. current   C. power   D. frequency

  38.____

39. Lock nuts are frequently used in making electrical connections on terminal boards. The purpose of such lock nuts is to

    A. make tighter connections with less effort
    B. make it difficult to tamper with the connections
    C. avoid stripping the threads
    D. keep the connections from loosening through vibration

  39.____

40. The core of an electro-magnet is USUALLY

    A. aluminum   B. lead   C. brass   D. iron

  40.____

41. A stranded wire is given the same size designation as a solid wire if it has the same

    A. cross-sectional area   B. weight per foot
    C. overall diameter   D. strength

  41.____

42. One advantage of cutting 1" rigid conduit with a hacksaw rather than a 3-wheel pipe cutter is that

    A. the cut can be made with less exertion
    B. the pipe is not squeezed out of round
    C. less reaming is required after the cut
    D. no vise is needed

  42.____

43. Assume that the field leads of a large, completely disconnected d.c. motor are not tagged or otherwise marked. You could readily tell the shunt field leads from the series field leads by the

    A. length of the leads
    C. thickness of insulation
    B. size of wire
    D. type of insulation

44. Standard electrician's pliers should NOT be used to

    A. bend thin sheet metal
    B. crush insulation on wires to be skinned
    C. cut off nail points sticking through a board
    D. hold a wire in position for soldering

45. The device used to change a.c. to d.c. is a

    A. frequency   B. regulator   C. transformer   D. rectifier

46. The CHIEF advantage of using stranded rather than solid conductors for electrical wiring is that stranded conductors are

    A. more flexible
    C. smaller
    B. easier to skin
    D. stronger

47. One identifying feature of a squirrel-cage induction motor is that it has no

    A. windings on the stationary part
    B. commutator or slip rings
    C. air gap
    D. iron core in the rotating part

48. If a cartridge fuse is hot to the touch when you remove it to do some maintenance on the circuit, this MOST probably indicates that the

    A. voltage of the circuit is too high
    B. fuse clips do not make good contact
    C. equipment on the circuit starts and stops frequently
    D. fuse is oversize for the circuit

49. The instrument MOST commonly used to determine the state of charge of a lead-acid storage battery is the

    A. thermometer
    C. voltmeter
    B. hydrometer
    D. ammeter

50. Rigid conduit must be installed as to prevent the collection of water in it between outlets. In order to meet this requirement, the conduit should NOT have a

    A. low point between successive outlets
    B. high point between successive outlets
    C. low point at an outlet
    D. high point at an outlet

KEY (CORRECT ANSWERS)

1. C	11. D	21. C	31. B	41. A
2. D	12. C	22. B	32. D	42. C
3. D	13. D	23. D	33. D	43. B
4. A	14. B	24. A	34. A	44. C
5. B	15. A	25. C	35. B	45. D
6. D	16. C	26. C	36. B	46. A
7. D	17. A	27. C	37. D	47. B
8. B	18. D	28. A	38. A	48. B
9. A	19. B	29. B	39. D	49. B
10. C	20. C	30. B	40. D	50. A

TEST 3

DIRECTIONS: Each question or incomplete statement is followed by several suggested answers or completions. Select the one that *BEST* answers the question or completes the statement. *PRINT THE LETTER OF THE CORRECT ANSWER IN THE SPACE AT THE RIGHT.*

1. When a test lamp is connected to the two ends of a cartridge fuse on an operating switchboard, the indication in ALL cases will be that this fuse is

    A. blown if the test lamp remains dark
    B. good if the test lamp lights
    C. blown if the test lamp lights
    D. good if the test lamp remains dark

1____

2. If one copper wire has a diameter of 0.128 inch, and another copper wire has a diameter of 0.064 inch, the resistance of 1,000 feet of the first wire compared to the same length of the second wire is

    A. one half   B. one quarter   C. double   D. four times

2____

3. If the allowable current in a copper bus bar is 1,000 amperes per square inch of cross-section, the width of a standard 1/4" bus bar designed to carry 1500 amperes would be

    A. 2"   B. 4"   C. 6"   D. 8"

3____

4. It is not possible to obtain a 200-watt light-bulb that is as small in all dimensions as the standard 150-watt light-bulb.
    The PRINCIPAL advantage to users resulting from this reduction in size is that

    A. maintenance electricians can carry many more light-bulbs
    B. two sizes of light-bulbs can be kept in the same storage space
    C. the higher wattage bulb can now fit into certain lighting fixtures
    D. less breakage is apt to occur in handling

4____

5. A carbon brush in a d.c. motor should exert a pressure of about 1 1/2 lbs. per square inch on the commutator.
    A much lighter pressure would be MOST likely to result in

    A. sparking at the commutator
    B. vibration of the armature
    C. the brush getting out of line
    D. excessive wear of the brush holder

5____

6. The number of watts of heat given off by a resistor is expressed by the formula I^2R.
    If 10 volts is applied to a 5-ohm resistor, the heat given off will be _____ watts.

    A. 500   B. 250   C. 50   D. 20

6____

7. When a number of rubber insulated wires are being pulled into a run of conduit having several sharp bends between the two pull boxes, the pulling is likely to be hard and the wires are subjected to considerable strain.
    For these reasons it is ADVISABLE in such a case to

7____

A. push the wires into the feed end of the conduit at the same time that pulling is being done
B. pull in only one wire at a time
C. use extra heavy grease
D. pull the wires back a few inches after each forward pull to gain momentum

8. The plug of a portable tool should be removed from the convenience outlet by grasping the plug and not by pulling on the cord because   8._____

A. the plug is easier to grip than the cord
B. pulling on the cord may allow the plug to fall on the floor and break
C. pulling on the cord may break the wires off the plug terminals
D. the plug is generally better insulated than the cord

9. When using a pipe wrench, the hand should be placed so as to pull instead of push on the wrench.   9._____
The basis for this recommendation is that there is less likelihood of

A. the wrench slipping
B. injury to the hand if the wrench slips
C. injury to the pipe if the wrench slips
D. stripped pipe threads

10. High voltage switches in power plants are commonly so constructed that their contacts are submerged in oil.   10._____
The purpose of the oil is to

A. help quench arcing
B. lubricate the contacts
C. cool the switch mechanism
D. insulate the contacts from the switch framework

11. In a storage battery installation consisting of twenty 2-volt cells connected in series, a leak develops in one of the cells and all the electrolyte runs out of it.   11._____
The terminal voltage across the twenty cells will now be

A. 40   B. 38   C. 2   D. 0

12. When removing the insulation from a wire before making a splice, care should be taken to avoid nicking the wire MAINLY because then the   12._____

A. current carrying capacity will be reduced
B. resistance will be increased
C. insulation will be harder to remove
D. wire is more likely to break

13. Good practice dictates that an adjustable open-end wrench should be used PRIMARILY when the   13._____

A. nut to be turned is soft and must not be scored
B. proper size of fixed wrench is not available
C. extra leverage is needed
D. location is cramped permitting only a small turning angle

14. It would generally be poor practice to use ordinary slip-joint pliers to

    A.   pull a small nail   B.   bend a wire
    C.   remove a cotter pin   D.   tighten a machine bolt

15. The a.c. motor which has exactly the same speed at full-load as at no load is the _____ motor.

    A.   synchronous   B.   repulsion   C.   induction   D.   condenser

16. A metal bushing is usually screwed on to the end of rigid conduit inside of a junction box. The bushing serves to

    A.   center the wires in the conduit
    B.   separate the wires where they leave the conduit
    C.   protect the wires against abrasion
    D.   prevent sagging of the conduit

17. The PROPER abrasive for cleaning the commutator of a d.c. generator is

    A.   steel wool   B.   emery cloth   C.   sand paper   D.   soapstone

18. If a *live* 120-volt d.c. lighting circuit is connected to the 120-volt winding of an otherwise disconnected power transformer, the result will be

    A.   blowing of the d.c. circuit fuse
    B.   magnetization of the transformer fuse
    C.   sparking at the transformer secondary terminals
    D.   burning out of lights on the d.c. circuit

19. Threaded joints in rigid conduit runs are made watertight through the use

    A.   petroleum jelly   B.   solder   C.   red lead   D.   paraffin wax

20. The letters S.P.S.T. frequently found on wiring plans refer to a type of

    A.   cable   B.   switch   C.   fuse   D.   motor

21. Renewable fuses differ from ordinary fuses in that

    A.   they can carry higher overloads
    B.   burned out fuses can be located more easily
    C.   burned out fuse elements can be readily replaced
    D.   they can be used on higher voltages

22. After No. 10 A.W.G., the next SMALLER copper wire size in common use is No.

    A. 8   B. 9   C. 11   D. 12

23. The BEST of the following tools to use for cutting off a piece of single-conductor #6 rubber insulated lead covered cable is

    A.   pair of electrician's pliers   B.   hacksaw
    C.   hammer and cold chisel   D.   lead knife

24. Toggle bolts are MOST appropriate for use to fasten conduit clamps to a   24.____

    A.   steel column   B.   concrete wall
    C.   hollow tile wall   D.   brick wall

25. If a 10-24 by 3/4" machine screw is not available, the screw which could be MOST easily modified to use in an emergency is a   25.____

    A.   10-24 by 1/2"   B.   12-24 by 3/4"
    C.   10-24 by 1 1/2"   D.   8-24 by 3/4"

26. A standard pipe thread differs from a standard screw thread in that the pipe thread   26.____

    A.   is tapered
    B.   is deeper
    C.   requires no lubrication when cutting
    D.   has the same pitch for any diameter of pipe

27. The material which is LEAST likely to be found in use as the outer covering of rubber insulated wires or cables is   27.____

    A.   cotton   B.   varnished cambric
    C.   lead   D.   neoprene

28. In measuring to determine the size of a stranded insulated conductor, the proper place to use the wire gauge is on   28.____

    A.   the insulation   B.   the outer covering
    C.   the stranded conductor D.   one strand of the conductor

29. Rubber insulation on an electrical conductor would MOST quickly be damaged by continuous contact with   29.____

    A.   acid   B.   water   C.   oil   D.   alkali

30. If a fuse clip becomes hot under normal circuit load, the MOST probable cause is that the   30.____

    A.   clip makes poor contact with the fuse ferrule
    B.   circuit wires are too small
    C.   current rating of the fuse is too high
    D.   voltage rating of the fuse is too low

31. If the input of a 10 to 1 step-down transformer is 15 amperes at 2400 volts, the secondary output would be NEAREST to _____ amperes at _____ volts.   31.____

    A.   1.5; 24,000   B.   150; 240   C.   1.5; 240   D.   150; 24,000

32. The resistance of a copper wire to the flow of electricity   32.____

    A.   *increases* as the diameter of the wire increases
    B.   *decreases* as the diameter of the wire decreases
    C.   *decreases* as the length of the wire increases
    D.   *increases* as the length of the wire increases

33. Where galvanized steel conduit is used, the PRIMARY purpose of the galvanizing is to   3

    A. increase mechanical strength
    B. retard rusting
    C. provide a good surface for painting
    D. provide good electrical contact for grounding

34. The CORRECT method of measuring the power taken by an a.c electric motor is to use a   3

    A. wattmeter   B. voltmeter and an ammeter
    C. power factor meter   D. tachometer

35. Checking a piece of rigid electrical conduit with a steel scale, you measure the inside   3
    diameter as 1 1/16" and the outside diameter as 1 5/16".
    The NOMINAL size of this conduit is

    A. 3/4"   B. 1"   C. 1 1/4"   D. 1 1/2"

36. Of the following, it would be MOST difficult to solder a copper wire to a metal plate made   3
    of

    A. copper   B. brass   C. iron   D. tin

37. After a piece of rigid conduit has been cut to length, it is MOST important to   3

    A. ream the inside edge to prevent injury to wires
    B. file the end flat to make an accurate fit
    C. coat the cut surface with red lead to prevent rust
    D. rile the outside edge to a taper for ease in threading

38. Rigid conduit is generally secured to sheet metal outlet boxes by means of   3

    A. threadless couplings   B. box connectors
    C. locknuts and bushings   D. conduit clamps

39. While a certain d.c. shunt motor is driving a light load, part of the field winding becomes   3
    short circuited,
    The motor will MOST likely

    A. increase its speed   B. decrease its speed
    C. remain at the same speed   D. come to a stop

40. Each time a certain electric heater is turned on, the incandescent lights connected to the   4
    same branch circuit become dimmer and when the heater is turned off the lamps
    become brighter.
    The factor which probably contributes MOST to this effect is the

    A. voltage of the circuit   B. size of the circuit fuse
    C. current taken by the lamps   D. size of the circuit conductors

41. Comparing the shunt field winding with the series field winding of a compound d.c. motor,   4
    it would be CORRECT to say that the shunt field winding has _____ resistance,

    A. *more* turns but the *lower*   B. *more* turns and the *higher*
    C. *fewer* turns and the *lower*   D. *fewer* turns but the *higher*

42. The most important reason for using a fuse-puller when removing a cartridge fuse from the fuse clips is to   42._____

    A.   prevent blowing of the fuse
    B.   prevent injury to the fuse element
    C.   reduce the chances of personal injury
    D.   reduce arcing at the fuse clips

43. A coil of wire wound on an iron core draws exactly 5 amperes when connected across the terminals of a ten-volt storage battery.   43._____
If this coil is now connected across the ten-volt secondary terminals of an ordinary power transformer, the current drawn will be

    A.   *less* than 5 amperes
    B.   *more* than 5 amperes
    C.   *exactly* 5 amperes
    D.   more or less than 5 amperes depending on the frequency

44. A revolution counter applied to the end of a rotating shaft reads 100 when a stop-watch is started. It reads 850 when the stop-watch indicates 90 seconds.   44._____
The average RPM of the shaft is

    A. 8.4   B. 9.4   C. 500   D. 567

45. Motor speeds are generally measured directly in RPM by the use of a   45._____

    A. potentiometer   B. manometer   C. dynamometer   D. tachometer

46. To reverse the direction of rotation of a 3-phase motor, it is necessary to   46._____

    A.   increase the resistance of the rotor circuit
    B.   interchange any two of the three line connections
    C.   interchange all three line connections
    D.   reverse the polarity of the rotor circuit

47. Mica is commonly used in electrical construction for   47._____

    A.   commutator bar separators   B.   switchboard panels
    C.   strain insulators   D.   heater cord insulation

48. The rating term *1000 ohms, 10 watts* would generally be applied to a   48._____

    A. heater   B. relay   C. resistor   D. transformer

49. According to the National Electrical Code, the identified (or grounded) conductor of the branch circuit supplying an incandescent lamp socket must be connected to the screw shell.   49._____
The MOST likely reason for this requirement is that

    A.   longer lamp life results
    B.   the wiring will be kept more nearly uniform
    C.   persons are more likely to come in contact with the shell
    D.   the shell can carry heavier currents

50. In an installation used to charge a storage battery from a motor-generator you would
     LEAST expect to find a(n)

    A. rectifier   B. rheostat   C. voltmeter   D. ammeter

KEY (CORRECT ANSWERS)

1. C	11. D	21. C	31. B	41. B
2. B	12. D	22. D	32. D	42. C
3. C	13. B	23. B	33. B	43. A
4. C	14. D	24. C	34. A	44. C
5. A	15. A	25. C	35. B	45. D
6. D	16. C	26. A	36. C	46. B
7. A	17. C	27. B	37. A	47. A
8. C	18. A	28. D	38. C	48. C
9. B	19. C	29. C	39. A	49. C
10. A	20. B	30. A	40. D	50. A

ELECTRICITY
EXAMINATION SECTION

DIRECTIONS FOR THIS SECTION:
Each question or incomplete statement is followed by several suggested answers or completions. Select the one that *BEST* answers the question or completes the statement. *PRINT THE LETTER OF THE CORRECT ANSWER IN THE SPACE AT THE RIGHT.*

TEST 1

1. The *one* of the following items in which the metal alloy   1. ...
   "Alnico" is *most likely* to be found is
   A. thermocouples   B. heating elements
   C. wire-wound resistors   D. permanent magnets
2. Of the following devices, the *one* which, when inserted be-   2. ...
   tween a rectifier and its load, *reduces* the ripple current
   is the
   A. wave trap   B. coupling transformer
   C. inverter   D. filter
3. The Q-factor (quality factor) of an inductor *equals* the   3. ...
   A. product of its reactance and its resistance
   B. product of its inductance and its resistance
   C. ratio of its inductance to its resistance
   D. ratio of its reactance to its resistance
4. Of the following types of screw heads, the *one* which re-   4. ...
   quires a cross-slot screw driver having 45-degree flukes
   and a sharp pointed head, is the
   A. Phillips   B. Recessed
   C. Torque-set   D. Reed and Prince
5. Of the following, the *most likely* reason why loudspeakers   5. ...
   in a public address system might produce a loud, howling
   noise when the input is a normal speaking voice, is
   A. feedback   B. attenuation
   C. squelching   D. transient current
6. A megohmmeter of suitable voltage is used to test the   6. ...
   condition of an A.C. electrolytic capacitor. Two readings
   are taken and the test leads are reversed between readings.
   The capacitor is discharged before and after the readings.
   The meter indications will *stabilize* at readings which are
   A. zero for one connection and high for the other, if the
      capacitor is defective
   B. high for one connection and zero for the other, if the
      capacitor is good
   C. zero for both connections, if the capacitor is good
   D. high for both connections, if the capacitor is good
7. Of the following terms, the *one* which is *most frequently*   7. ...
   used to describe circuits formed by etching metal foil de-
   posited on a base of insulating material is the
   A. printed circuit   B. wired circuit
   C. bread-board circuit   D. prototype circuit
8. The *PRIMARY* function of a "zero sequence" current trans-   8. ...
   former, when installed in a four-wire A.C. power distribution system, is to detect
   A. ground faults   B. metering errors
   C. phase sequences   D. power factors

1

9. In three-phase rectifier systems, it is *common practice*   9. ..
   to connect the power transformer with its *primaries* in
       A. delta and its *secondaries* in delta
       B. delta and its *secondaries* in wye
       C. wye and its *secondaries* in delta
       D. wye and its *secondaries* in wye
10. The tap changer in a distribution transformer is *normally*   10. ..
    used to change the
        A. voltage ratio   B. insulating oil
        C. winding polarity   D. impedance matching
11. The eddy currents in a distribution transformer can *BEST*   11. ..
    be reduced by
        A. laminating the iron core B. polarizing both windings
        C. installing a secondary capacitor
        D. increasing the primary voltage
12. Of the following procedures, the *one* which is a precaution 12. ..
    that should be taken when working with an instrument cur-
    rent transformer is:
        A. Short the primary before disconnecting it
        B. Short the secondary before disconnecting it
        C. Ground the primary after disconnecting it
        D. Ground the secondary after disconnecting it
13. If the line voltages across the load equal the phase volt- 13. ..
    ages across the load in a balanced three-phase A.C. circuit,
    the load is connected in
        A. delta   B. Scott   C. star   D. wye
14. Of the following motors, the *one MOST COMMONLY* used to   14. ..
    correct a lagging power factor is the
        A. induction motor   B. synchronous motor
        C. series motor   D. compound motor
15. The *one* of the following motors which *frequently* requires 15. ..
    a D.C. supply for excitation is the
        A. capacitor motor   B. shaded-pole motor
        C. wound-rotor motor   D. synchronous motor
16. Of the following, the *most likely* reason why a compound   16. ..
    D.C. motor is running more slowly at full load than it
    normally does is that its
        A. line voltage is too high
        B. series field bucks the shunt field
        C. shunt field is open   D. armature has a short
17. Suppose a newly installed D.C. shunt motor rotates in   17. ..
    the wrong direction. This condition can be *corrected*
    by reversing the connections to
        A. the armature and the field only
        B. either the armature or the field
        C. the armature, the field, and the line
        D. the line only
18. Switches used to disconnect generator or synchronous   18. ..
    motor fields are frequently designed to connect which of
    the following? A discharge
        A. *resistor* across the commutator before opening the circuit
        B. *capacitor* across the commutator after opening the circuit
        C. *capacitor* across the field after opening the circuit
        D. *resistor* across the field before opening the circuit

19. After grinding a new surface on a commutator having mica- 19. ...
insulated copper bars, it is *good practice* to
    A. side-cut the bars and under-cut the mica
    B. feather-edge the bars and create mica fins
    C. under-cut the bars and side-cut the mica
    D. dress both the bars and the mica until they are
       flush with each other

20. In a lap-wound D.C. motor armature, the two ends of each 20. ...
armature coil are *usually* connected to commutator segments
that are
    A. adjacent to each other   B. opposite from each other
    C. separated by 90 electrical degrees
    D. separated by 360 electrical degrees

TEST 2

1. The direction of rotation of an A.C. repulsion motor can   1. ...
be *reversed* by
    A. reversing the line connections
    B. reversing the field connections
    C. shifting the shading coil past the main stator winding
    D. shifting the brushes to the reverse side of the neutral

2. The number of threads per inch *usually* found on the   2. ...
threaded section of a 1-inch micrometer caliper's spindle, is
    A. 25   B. 40   C. 75   D. 100

3. Three-phase A.C. motors with six leads, when connected to 3. ...
star-delta starters, are usually *run*
    A. delta and *started* star   B. delta and *started* delta
    C. star and *started* delta   D. star and *started* star

4. In a typical three-phase A.C. electrically-operated   4. ...
magnetic motor starter, the auxiliary contact, the start
button, and the stop button are usually connected *so that*
the auxiliary contact is in
    A. *series* with both buttons B. *series* with the start button
    C. *parallel* with both buttons
    D. *parallel* with the start button

5. Of the following classifications of insulating materials 5. ...
used in electrical machinery, the *one* with the *HIGHEST
MAXIMUM* safe-operating temperature is class
    A. A   B. B   C. H   D. O

6. Of the following features, the *one* which makes it possible 6. ...
to operate certain circuit breakers *remotely*, regardless of
load, is the
    A. shunt trip   B. gutter tap
    C. limiter lug   D. thermal element

7. Thermal magnetic circuit breakers *usually* provide   7. ...
    A. *instantaneous* overload protection and *instantaneous*
       short circuit protection
    B. *inverse* time delay overload protection and *instantane-*
       ous short circuit protection
    C. *inverse* time delay overload protection and *inverse*
       time delay short circuit protection
    D. *instantaneous* overload protection and *inverse* time
       delay short circuit protection

8. Following are sets of branch circuit numbers for an 18-   8. ..
circuit, sequence-phased, lighting panelboard equipped
with single-phase circuit breakers in each circuit and
connected to a three-phase, four-wire feeder.
The set which consists of circuit numbers which are
usually *all* connected to the same phase is
    A. 1, 2, 3, 4, 5, 6   B. 1, 3, 5, 7, 9, 11
    C. 2, 4, 6, 8, 10, 12   D. 1, 2, 7, 8, 13, 14

9. Unless otherwise specified, lighting panelboard boxes are   9. ..
usually manufactured with knockouts *only* on the
    A. top, bottom, and back   B. top, and both sides
    C. bottom, and both sides   D. top and bottom

10. When using a 12-point box wrench to turn a nut, the   10. ..
MINIMUM angle through which the wrench must be swung
before the next set of points can be fitted to the corners
of the nut, is
    A. 15°   B. 30°   C. 45°   D. 60°

11. Suppose that the floor plans for a certain building are   11. ..
drawn to a scale of 1/8" = 1'0". On these plans the
distance between two symbols representing receptacle
outlets measures 2 7/8" on an ordinary ruler.
The *actual* distance between the two receptacle outlets
installed at these locations should be
    A. 2 7/8 inches   B. 2 feet 7 inches
    C. 16 feet   D. 23 feet

12. Of the following combinations of switches, the one *usually*   12. ..
used when it is necessary to control a lighting fixture
from five different locations, is
    A. two three-way switches and three four-way switches
    B. two four-way switches and three three-way switches
    C. five three-way switches   D. five four-way switches

13. Of the following, the *most common* use for a Wheatstone   13. ..
bridge is to
    A. shunt leakage currents   B. measure resistances
    C. bypass faulty components D. support scaffolds

14. Suppose that, when both test-tips of a neon-glow lamp   14. ..
tester are properly placed across a live circuit, only one
of its electrodes glows. Of the following, the *most likely*
reason for this is that the circuit is
    A. D.C., and the glowing electrode is connected to the
       negative side
    B. D.C., and the glowing electrode is connected to the
       positive side
    C. A.C., and the voltage is too low to permit both
       electrodes to glow
    D. A.C., and the glowing electrode is connected to the
       grounded neutral

15. The specific gravity of a fully charged lead acid storage   15. ..
battery is, *most nearly*,
    A. 1.000   B. 1.150   C. 1.280   D. 1.830

16. The three regions in a junction transistor cross-section   16. ..
are *commonly* known as the
    A. cathode, grid, and emitter regions
    B. collector, emitter, and base regions
    C. base, grid, and plate regions
    D. emitter, cathode, and screen regions

17. An axially color-coded fixed resistor, having neither a   17. ...
    gold nor a silver marking, is *only accurate TO WITHIN*
    A. 5 percent of its marked value
    B. 10 percent of its marked value
    C. 15 percent of its marked value
    D. 20 percent of its marked value

18. Of the following sizes of machine screws, the *one* indicat- 18. ...
    ing the *GREATEST* number of threads per inch, is the
    A. No. 6 - 32   B. No. 10 - 24
    C. No. 14 - 18   D. No. 30 - 14

19 The number of threads per inch *most commonly* used on 3/4 19. ...
    inch rigid conduit is
    A. 27   B 18   C. 14   D. 8

20 Of the following three-phase, 4-wire, secondary voltage   20. ...
    combinations, the *one most frequently* used in industrial
    plants and commercial buildings, is
    A. 138/240 volts   B. 208/260 volts
    C. 277/480 volts   D. 347/600 volts

TEST 3

1. The *total resistance* of ten 5-ohm resistors connected in   1. ...
   parallel is
   A. 50 ohms   B. 10 ohms   C. 2 ohms   D. 0.5 ohm

2. The power consumed by a 100-ohm resistor carrying a D.C.   2. ...
   current of 5 amperes is
   A. 4 watts   B. 20 watts   C. 500 watts   D. 2500 watts

3. The impedance of a series circuit consisting of a 6-ohm   3. ...
   resistor, a 12-ohm capacitive reactance, and a 4-ohm
   inductive reactance, is
   A. 22 ohms   B. 18 ohms   C. 16 ohms   D. 10 ohms

4. The capacitive reactance of a 60-Hertz A.C. circuit con-   4. ...
   sisting of a 50 microfarad capacitor is, *most nearly,*
   A. .0188 ohm   B. .0200 ohm   C. 53 ohms   D. 3,000 ohms

5. A coil having an inductive reactance of 100 ohms is de-   5. ...
   signed to operate satisfactorily at 120 volts and 60 Hertz.
   This coil has negligible resistance and is energized from a
   120-volt, 25-Hertz source. In order not to exceed rated
   current, it will be necessary to add a resistance in series
   with the coil.
   The *value* of this resistance is, *most nearly,*
   A. 40 ohms   B. 60 ohms   C. 80 ohms   D. 100 ohms

6. The power factor of a single-phase A.C. circuit consuming   6. ...
   1,800 watts at 120 volts while drawing 20 amperes, is
   A. .50   B. .75   C. .86   D. 1.33

7. The *MAXIMUM* instantaneous voltage that occurs across a   7. ...
   circuit which is connected to a common 120-volt, 60-Hertz,
   single-phase supply, is, *most nearly,*
   A. 120 volts   B. 141 volts   C. 170 volts   D. 208 volts

8. The line current in a three-phase, four-wire 120/208 volt   8. ...
   feeder circuit, supplying a balanced 120-volt lighting load
   totaling 36 kilowatts, is, *most nearly,*
   A. 300 amps   B. 173 amps   C. 100 amps   D. 57 amps

5

9. Three equal resistors connected in delta across a three-phase, 120/208 volt supply, drawing line currents of 30 amperes, will *each* have a resistance of, *most nearly,*
  A. 4 ohms   B. 12 ohms   C. 33 ohms   D. 70 ohms

9. ...

10. The *full load-line current* of a squirrel cage induction motor rated at 2 H.P., having an efficiency of 70%, a power factor of 70%, and connected to a 3-phase, 208-volt, 60-Hertz supply, is, *most nearly,*
  A. 1.5 amperes   B. 5.0 amperes
  C. 8.5 amperes   D. 14.5 amperes

10. ...

11. A D.C. circuit consists of an unknown resistance in series with a five-ohm resistor. It is found that when a voltmeter is placed across the five-ohm resistor, it reads 40 volts.
  If the voltmeter reads 54 volts when placed across the unknown resistance, the *value* of the unknown resistance is, *most nearly,*
  A. 3.7 ohms   B. 6.8 ohms   C. 7.0 ohms   D. 14.0 ohms

11. ...

12. If the diameter of a copper wire is twice the diameter of another copper wire of the same length, the resistance of the *first wire* will be
  A. 1/4 of the resistance of the *second wire*
  B. 1/2 of the resistance of the *second wire*
  C. 2 times the resistance of the *second wire*
  D. 4 times the resistance of the *second wire*

12. ...

13. A defective 120-volt, 1-kilowatt electric heater needs a new heating element. If this element is to consist of a continuous length of nichrome wire having a resistance of 1.5 ohms per foot, the length of this wire should be, *most nearly,*
  A. 3.5 feet   B. 8.5 feet   C. 9.5 feet   D. 14.5 feet

13. ...

14. The diameter of a round copper bus-bar having a circular cross-section with an area of 250,000 circular mils, is, *most nearly,*
  A. 1/4 inch   B. 1/2 inch   C. 2 1/2 inches D. 5 inches

14. ...

15. The number of circular mils in a copper wire whose diameter is 1/8" is, *most nearly,*
  A. 125,000   B. 15,625   C. 3,140   D. 387

15. ...

16. A 2"-wide rectangular copper bus-bar is to carry 500 amperes D.C. without exceeding a maximum allowable current density of 1,000 amperes. The *MINIMUM* thickness of this bus-bar must be
  A. 1/8 inch   B. 3/16 inch   C. 1/4 inch   D. 1/2 inch

16. ...

17. A three-phase, 60-Hertz A.C. squirrel cage induction motor will have a synchronous speed of 1200 rpm if it has
  A. 4 poles   B. 6 poles   C. 8 poles   D. 10 poles

17. ...

18. The speed of a four-pole, three-phase, 60-Hertz, squirrel cage induction motor running with a slip of 5.6% will be, *most nearly,*
  A. 850 rpm   B. 1700 rpm   C. 2550 rpm   D. 3400 rpm

18. ...

19. The full load-line current of a 1-horsepower, single-phase, 60-Hertz, A.C. motor, having an efficiency of 70 percent, is, *most nearly,*
  A. 4 amperes   B. 6 amperes   C. 8 amperes   D. 10 amperes

19. ...

20. The percent regulation of a single-phase transformer whose 20. ...
secondary terminal voltage varies from 126 volts at no
load, to 120 volts at full load, is, *most nearly*,
   A. 3.6 percent   B. 4.8 percent
   C. 5.0 percent   D. 6.0 percent

———

TEST 4

1. When preparing fresh electrolyte for a lead-acid storage   1. ...
battery, it is considered best to pour the concentrated
acid into the water rather than adding water to the concentrated acid. The *MAIN* reason for following this sequence
is to prevent
   A. corrosion   B. sedimentation
   C. loss of concentrated acid
   D. production of excessive heat
2. Fire extinguishers suitable for use on an electrical fire   2. ...
should be identified by a
   A. five-pointed star containing the letter "D"
   B. triangle containing the letter "A"
   C. square containing the letter "B"
   D. circle containing the letter "C"
3. The *SMALLEST* size of rigid conduit that may be installed   3. ...
when wiring for new branch circuit receptacle outlets is
   A. 1 inch   B. 3/4 inch   C. 1/2 inch   D. 3/8 inch
4. Of the following, the *color* of a fixed equipment ground   4. ...
wire should be
   A. white   B. black   C. red   D. green
5. Of the following, the *HEAVIEST* fixture that may be sup-   5. ...
ported *directly* from its outlet box is one weighing
   A. 25 pounds   B. 35 pounds   C. 45 pounds   D. 55 pounds
6. The *SMALLEST* size of copper wire that may be used as a   6. ...
system ground on an A.C. service is
   A. No. 6   B. No. 8   C. No. 10   D. No. 12
7. The *SMALLEST* size of feeder conductor that must be stranded 7. ...
if installed in raceways is
   A. No. 6   B. No. 2   C. No. 1/0   D. 250 MCM
8. Of the following locations, the *ones* usually classified as 8. ...
Class I hazardous locations are
   A. rooms used for spray painting   B. woodworking plants
   C. cotton-waste storage rooms   D. janitor's sink closets
9. In relation to the allowable current carrying capacity of   9. ...
wiring it is protecting, the *MAXIMUM VALUE* that an instantaneous magnetic trip circuit breaker may be set for is
____ of the allowable current-carrying capacity.
   A. 75%   B. 100%   C. 125%   D. 150%
10. When installed in vertical raceways, 500 MCM feeders must   10. ...
be supported at intervals *NOT* greater than
   A. 100 feet   B. 75 feet   C. 50 feet   D. 25 feet
11. Sections of existing conduit exceeding 3 feet in length   11. ...
are being used to rewire for increased load, using more
than four non-lead covered conductors. The *MAXIMUM PER-
CENTAGE* of the conduit's cross-sectional area which may be

occupied by these conductors is
    A. 60%   B. 50%   C. 40%   D. 30%

12. The *MAXIMUM LENGTH* of armored cable that may be exposed   12. ...
at the terminal connections of a ventilating fan located
in a fan room is
    A. 8 feet   B. 6 feet   C. 4 feet   D. 2 feet

13. The *MAXIMUM ALLOWABLE CURRENT RATING* for a 250-volt, fer-   13. ...
rule contact, cartridge fuse is
    A. 200 amperes B. 100 amperes C. 60 amperes D. 30 amperes

14. An approved attachment plug and receptacle may be used as   14. ...
the controller for a portable motor whose horsepower rating
is *NOT* larger than
    A. 1/4 HP   B. 1/3 HP   C. 1/2 HP   D. 1 HP

15. A printed or typed directory must be mounted in an ap-   15. ...
proved manner on the door of a panelboard *having more than*
    A. 4 circuits B. 6 circuits C. 8 circuits D. 10 circuits

16. Surface metal raceways should *NOT* be used for wires   16. ...
larger than
    A. No. 6   B. No. 8   C. No. 10   D. No. 12

17. The *MINIMUM LENGTH* of a pull box with knockouts, installed 17. ...
in a run of 1 1/2-inch conduit containing a set of No. 4 RH
lighting panel feeders, is
    A. 24 inches B. 18 inches C. 12 inches D. 6 inches

18. Suppose you find some of the conductors in a cutout box   18. ...
identified by means of a half-inch wide band of yellow
tape. Of the following, it is *most likely* that these
identified conductors are in circuits that are
    A. direct current   B. alternating current
    C. grounded   D. spares

19. The *MINIMUM SIZE* of wire that may be used as fixture wire 19. ...
is
    A. No. 14   B. No. 16   C. No. 18   D. No. 20

20. The *SMALLEST SIZE* of copper wire that may be used as an   20. ...
equipment ground if the branch circuit over-current device
is rated at 20 amperes, is a
    A. No. 10   B. No. 12   C. No. 16   D. No. 18

KEYS (CORRECT ANSWERS)

TEST 1		TEST 2		TEST 3		TEST 4	
1. B	11. A	1. D	11. D	1. D	11. B	1. D	11. C
2. D	12. B	2. B	12. A	2. D	12. A	2. D	12. B
3. D	13. A	3. A	13. B	3. D	13. C	3. C	13. C
4. D	14. B	4. D	14. A	4. C	14. B	4. D	14. A
5. A	15. D	5. C	15. C	5. B	15. B	5. C	15. A
6. D	16. D	6. A	16. B	6. B	16. C	6. B	16. A
7. A	17. B	7. B	17. D	7. C	17. B	7. A	17. C
8. A	18. D	8. D	18. A	8. C	18. B	8. A	18. A
9. B	19. A	9. D	19. C	9. B	19. C	9. C	19. C
10. A	20. A	10. B	20. C	10. C	20. C	10. C	20. C

BASIC FUNDAMENTALS OF ELECTRICAL WIRING

TABLE OF CONTENTS

Basic Fundamentals Of Electrical Wiring

SECTION I. INTRODUCTION

1-1. PURPOSE AND SCOPE

These notes provide practical information in the basics and procedures of electrical wiring, a full exposition of the electrician's tools and equipment, and a description of the common components or general-use materials of the many different wiring systems currently in use which vary from the simple to the complex.

1-2. COMMENTARY

The student is encouraged to proceed on from this basic plateau to a study of specialized areas of the subject of interior wiring, such as design and layout, open wiring, cable wiring, and maintenance.

Section II. FUNDAMENTALS AND PROCEDURES OF ELECTRICAL WIRING

1-3. Fundamentals of Electricity

a. Throughout this part, emphasis is placed on the constructional aspects of electric wiring. Detailed coverage of electrical fundamentals may be found in standard text books .The term "phase" is used when refer ring to the angular displacement between two or more like quantities, either alternating electromotive force (EMF) or alternating currents. It is likewise used in distinguishing the different types of alternating current generators. For example, a machine designed to generate a single EMF wave is called a single-phase alternator, and one designed to generate two or more EMF waves is called a polyphase alternator.

b. Power generators will produce single or three-phase voltages that may be used for electrical power systems at generated voltages or through transformer systems.

(1) Single-phase generators are normally used only for small lighting and single-phase motor loads. If the generated voltage is 120 volts then a two-wire system is used, see table C-1(A). One of the conductors is grounded and the other is ungrounded or hot. The generated single-phase voltage may be 240 volts. This voltage is normally used for larger single-phase motors. In order to provide power for lighting loads, the 240-volt phase is center-tapped to provide a three-wire single-phase system, see table C-1(B). The center tap is the grounded neutral conductor. The voltage from this grounded conductor to either of the two ungrounded

ITEM	SYMBOL
WIRING CONCEALED IN CEILING OR WALL	
WIRING CONCEALED IN FLOOR	
EXPOSED BRANCH CIRCUIT	
BRANCH CIRCUIT HOME RUN TO PANEL BOARD (NO. OF ARROWS EQUALS NO. OF CIRCUITS, DESIGNATION IDENTIFIES DESIGNATION AT PANEL)	Al A3
THREE OR MORE WIRES (NO. OF CROSS LINES EQUALS NO. OF CONDUCTORS TWO CONDUCTORS INDICATED IF NOT OTHERWISE NOTED)	///
INCOMING SERVICE LINES	
CROSSED CONDUCTORS, NOT CONNECTED	OR
SPLICE OR SOLDERED CONNECTION	OR
CABLED CONNECTOR (SOLDERLESS)	
WIRE TURNED UP	
WIRE TURNED DOWN	

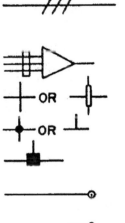

Figure 1-1. Standard electrical symbols (sheet 1).

(hot) conductors is 120 volts. This is one half of the total phase value. The voltage between the two ungrounded conductors is 240 volts. This system provides power for both lighting and single-phase 240-volt motors.

(2) The most common electrical system is the three-phase system. The generated EMF's are 120 degrees apart in phase. As shown in table C-1 (C, D, E), three-phase systems may be carried by three or four wires. If connected in a delta (A), the common phase voltage is 240 volts. Some systems generate 480 or 600 volts. If the delta has a grounded center tap neutral, then a voltage equal to one half the phase voltage is available. If the phases are wye (y) con-

nected then the phase voltage is equal to $\sqrt{3}$ (1.73) times the phase-to-neutral voltage. The most common electrical system found in the military is the three-phase four-wire 208/120 volt system.

c. Single-phase three-wire and three-phase four-wire systems provide voltages for both lighting and power loads. If the load between each of the three phases or between the two ungrounded conductors and their grounded center tapped neutral are equal, a balanced circuit exists. When this occurs there is no current flowing in the neutral conductor. Because of this, two ungrounded conductors and one grounded neutral may be used to feed two circuits.

COMMON SYMBOLS AND LINE CONVENTIONS USED IN WIRING PLANS

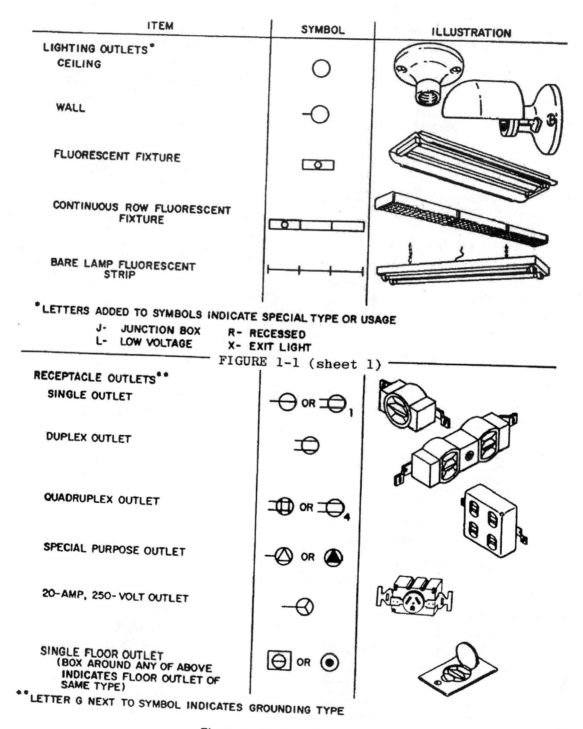

FIGURE 1-1 (sheet 1)

*LETTERS ADDED TO SYMBOLS INDICATE SPECIAL TYPE OR USAGE
J- JUNCTION BOX   R- RECESSED
L- LOW VOLTAGE   X- EXIT LIGHT

**LETTER G NEXT TO SYMBOL INDICATES GROUNDING TYPE

Figure 1-1—Continued (sheet 2)

Thus, three conductors may be used where otherwise four are normally required.

d. The preceding discussion leads logically into one-, two-, and three-phase electric light circuits. Electric lamps for indoor lighting in the United States are generally operated at 110 to 120 volts from constant-potential circuits. Two- and three-wire distri-

ITEM	SYMBOL	ILLUSTRATION
SWITCHES		
SINGLE POLE SWITCH	S	
DOUBLE POLE SWITCH	S_2	
THREE WAY SWITCH	S_3	
SWITCH AND PILOT LAMP	S_P	
CEILING PULL SWITCH	⑤	
PANEL BOARDS AND RELATED EQUIPMENT PANEL BOARD AND CABINET		
SWITCHBOARD, CONTROL STATION OR SUBSTATION		
SERVICE SWITCH OR CIRCUIT BREAKER	OR OR ⊗	
EXTERNALLY OPERATED DISCONNECT SWITCH		
MOTOR CONTROLLER	OR MC	
MISCELLANEOUS TELEPHONE	▶	
THERMOSTAT	Ⓣ	
MOTOR	Ⓜ	

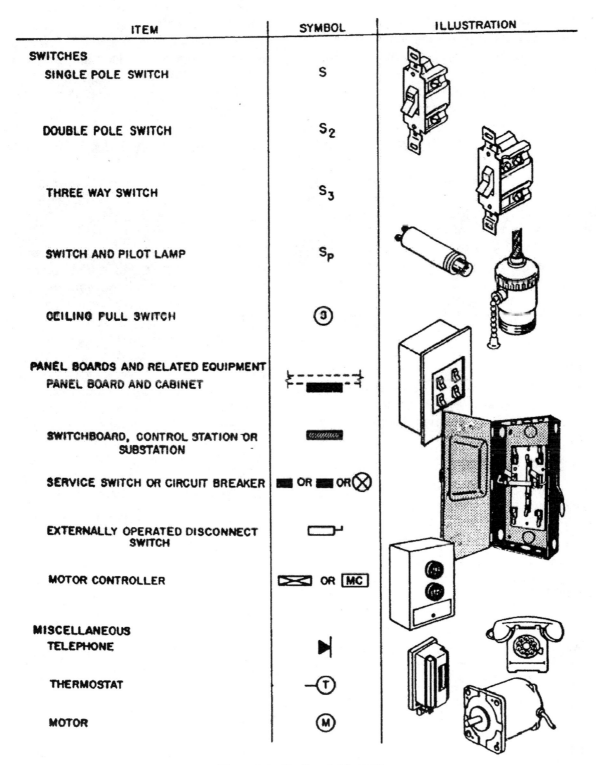

Figure 1-1—Continued (sheet 3)

bution systems, either direct current or single-phase alternating current, are widely used for lighting installations.

e. These systems of distribution are capable of handling both lamp and motor loads connected in parallel between the constant-potential lines. The three-wire system provides twice the potential difference between the outside wires than it does between either of the outside wires and the central or neutral wire. This system makes it possible to operate the larger motors at 240 volts while the lamps and smaller motors operate at 120 volts. When the load is unbalanced, a current in the neutral wire will correspond to the difference in current taken by the two sides. A balance of load is sought in laying out the wiring for lighting installations.

1-4. Drawing Symbols and Blueprint Reading

The electrician must be able to interpret simple blueprints since his construction orders will ordinarily be in that form. He needs the ability to make simple engineering sketches to describe work for which he receives only verbal orders.

a. Symbols. The more common symbols and line conventions used in wiring plans are shown in figure 1-1. These symbols enable precise location of any electrical equipment in a building from the study of a drawing.

b. Schematic Wiring Diagrams. Electrical plans show what items are to be installed, their approximate location, and the circuits to which they are to be connected. A typical electrical plan for a post exchange is shown in figure 1-2. The plan shows that the incoming service consists of three No. 8 wires and that two circuit-breaker panels are to be installed. Starting at the upper left, the plan shows that nine ceiling lighting outlets and two duplex wall outlets are to be installed in the bulk storage area. The arrow designated "B2" indicates that these outlets are to be connected to circuit 2 of circuit-breaker panel B. Note that three wires are indicated from this point to the double home-

run arrows designated "B1, B2." These are, the hot wire from the bulk storage area to circuit 2 of panel B, the hot wire from the administration area to circuit 1 of panel B, and a common neutral. The two hot conductors must be connected to different phases at the panel. This allows a cancellation of current in the neutral when both circuits are fully loaded (para 1-3c). From the double arrowhead, these wires are run to the circuit breaker panel without additional connections.

b. Schematic Wiring Diagrams. This is the form of wiring plans used most frequently for construction drawings (fig. 1-2). Single lines indicate the location of wires connecting the fixtures and equipment. Two conductors are indicated in a schematic diagram by a single line. If there are more than two wires together, short parallel lines through the line symbols indicate the number of wires represented by the line. Connecting wires are indicated by placing a dot at the point of intersection. No dot is used where wires cross without connecting. The electrician may encounter drawings in which the lines indicating the wiring have been omitted. In this type of drawing only the fixture and equipment symbols are shown; the location of the actual wiring is to be determined by the electrician. No actual dimensions or dimension lines are shown in electrical drawings. Location dimensions and spacing requirements are given in the form of notes or follow the standard installation principles shown in figure 1-1.

c. Drawing Notes. A list of drawing notes is ordinarily provided on a schematic wiring diagram to specify special wiring requirements and indicate building conditions which alter standard installation methods.

1-5. Color Coding

The National Electrical Code requires that a grounded or neutral conductor be identified by an outer color of white or natural gray for Number 6 wire or smaller. For larger conductors the outer identification of white or natural gray may be used, or they should be identified by white markings at the terminals. The ungrounded conductors of a circuit should be identified with insulation colored black, red, and blue, used in that order, in two-, three-, or four-wire circuits, respectively. All circuit conductors of the same color shall be connected to the same ungrounded (hot) feeder conductor throughout the installation. A grounding conductor, used solely for grounding purposes, should be bare or have a green covering.

1-6. Splices

A spliced wire must be as good a conductor as a continuous conductor. Figure 1-3 shows many of the variations of splicing used to obtain an electrically secure joint. Though

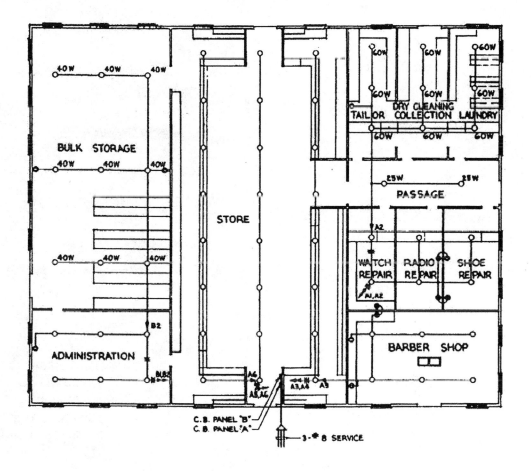

ELECTRICAL PLAN
SCALE NO. 1

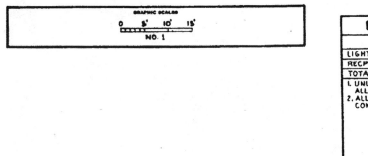

GRAPHIC SCALE
0   5'   10'   15'
NO. 1

ELECTRICAL NOTES	
CONNECTED LOAD	
LIGHTING	5.15 KW
RECP EST	1.20 KW
TOTAL	6.35 KW

1. UNLESS OTHERWISE NOTED ON PLAN ALL LAMPS TO BE 100W.
2. ALL 40, 60 & 100W LAMPS TO HAVE 8" CONICAL SHADES.

Figure 1-2. Typical wiring diagram.

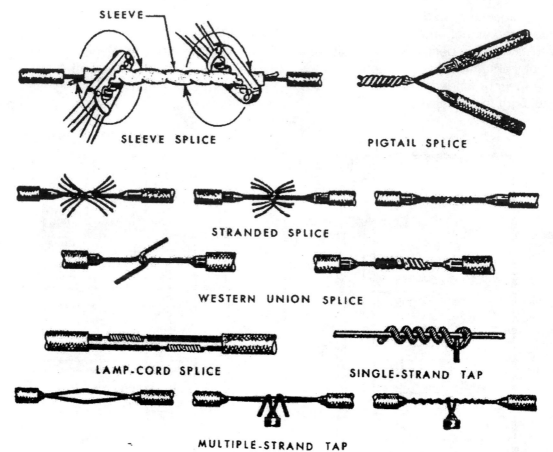

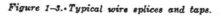

Figure 1–3.·Typical wire splices and taps.

splices are permitted wherever accessible in wiring systems, they should be avoided whenever possible. The best wiring practice (including open wiring systems) is to run continuous wires from the service box to the outlets. UNDER NO CONDITIONS SHOULD SPLICES BE PULLED THROUGH CONDUIT. SPLICES MUST BE PLACED IN APPROPRIATE ELECTRICAL BOXES.

1-7. Solderless Connectors

Figure 1-4 illustrates connectors used in place of splices because of their ease of installation. Since heavy wires are difficult to splice and solder properly, split-bolt connectors (1, fig. 1-4) are commonly used for wire joining. Solderless connectors, popularly called wire nuts, which are used for connecting small-gage and fixture wires, are illustrated in 2, figure 1-4. One design shown consists of a funnel-shaped metal-

spring insert molded into a plastic shell, into which the wires to be joined are screwed. The other type shown has a removable insert which contains a setscrew to clamp the wires. The plastic shell is screwed onto the insert to cover the joint.

1-8. Soldering

a. When a solderless connector is not used, the splice must be soldered before it is considered to be as good as the original conductor. The primary requirements for obtaining a good solder joint are a clean soldering iron, a clean joint, and a nonacid flux. These requirements can be satisfied by using pure rosin on the joint or by using a rosin core solder.

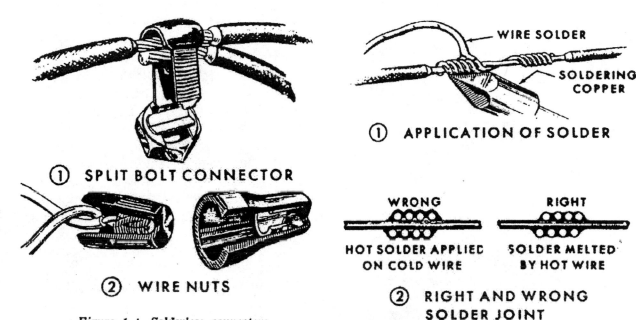

① SPLIT BOLT CONNECTOR

② WIRE NUTS

Figure 1–4. Solderless connectors.

① APPLICATION OF SOLDER

WRONG   RIGHT

HOT SOLDER APPLIED   SOLDER MELTED
ON COLD WIRE   BY HOT WIRE

② RIGHT AND WRONG
     SOLDER JOINT

Figure 1–5. Soldering and solder joints.

b. To insure a good solder joint, the electric heated or copper soldering iron should be applied to the joint (1, fig. 1-5) until the joint melts the solder by its own heat. Two, figure 1-5 shows the difference between a good and bad solder joint. The bad joint has a weak crystalline structure.

c. Figure 1-6 illustrates dip soldering. This method of soldering is frequently used by experienced electricians because of its convenience and relative speed for soldering pigtail splices.

1-9. Taping Joints

a. Every soldered joint must be covered with a coating of rubber, or varnished cambric, and friction tape to replace the wire insulation of the conductor. In taping a spliced solder joint (fig. 1-7), the rubber or cambric tape is started on the tapered end of the wire insulation and advances toward the other end, with each succeeding wrap, by overlapping the windings. This procedure is repeated from one end of the splice to the other until the original thickness has been restored. The joint is then covered with several layers of friction tape.

b. Though the method in a above for taping joints is still considered to be standard, the plastic electrical tape, which serves as an insulation and a protective covering, should be used whenever available. This tape materially reduces the time required to tape a joint and reduces the space needed by the joint because a satisfactory protective and insulation covering can be achieved with three-layer taping.

1-10. Insulation and Making Wire Con-nec-tions

a. When attaching a wire to a switch or an electrical device or when splicing it to another wire, the wire insulation must be removed to bare the copper conductor. One, figure 1-8 shows the right and wrong way to remove insulation. When the wire-stripping tool is applied at right angles to the wire, there is danger that the wire may be nicked and thus weakened. Therefore extreme caution must be used to make sure the wire is not nicked. To avoid nicks, the cut is made at an angle to the conductor. After the protective insulation is removed, the conductor is scraped or sanded thoroughly to remove all traces of insulation and oxide on the wire.

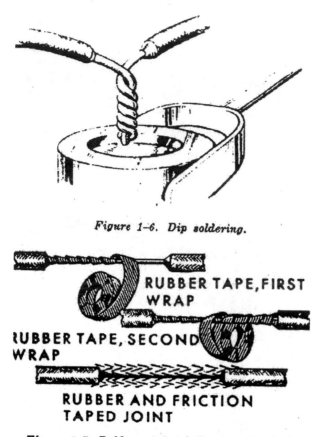

Figure 1-6. Dip soldering.

RUBBER TAPE, FIRST WRAP

RUBBER TAPE, SECOND WRAP

RUBBER AND FRICTION TAPED JOINT

Figure 1-7. Rubber- and friction-tape insulating.

b. Two and three, figure 1-8 show the correct method of attaching the trimmed wire to terminals. The wire loop is always inserted under the terminal screw, as shown, so that tightening the screw tends to close the loop. The loop is made so that the wire insulation ends close to the terminal.

1-11. Job Sequence

a. *Scope.* The installation of interior wiring is generally divided into two major divisions called roughing-in and finishing. Roughing-in is the installation of the outlet boxes, cable, wire, and conduit. Finishing is the installation of the switches, receptacles, covers, fixtures, and the completion of the service. The interval between these two work periods is used by other trades for plastering, enclosing walls, finishing floors, and trimming.

b. *Roughing-in.*

(1) The first step in the roughing-in phase of a wiring job is the mounting of out-

let boxes. The mounting can be expedited if the locations of all boxes are first marked on the studs and joists of the building.

(2) All the boxes are mounted on the building members on their own or by special brackets. For concealed installation, all boxes must be installed with the forward edge or plaster ring of the boxes flush with the finished walls.

(3) The circuiting and installation of wire for open wiring, cable, or conduit should be the next step. This involves the drilling and cutting-out of the building members to allow for the passage of the conductor or its protective covering. The production-line method of drilling the holes for all runs (as the installations between boxes are called) at one time, and then installing all of the wire, cable, or conduit, will expedite the job.

(4) The final roughing-in step in the installation of conduit systems is the pulling-in of wires between boxes. This can also be included as the first step in the finishing phase and requires care in the handling of the wires to prevent the marring of finished wall or floor surfaces.

c. Finishing.

(1) The splicing of joints in the outlet and junction boxes and the connection of the bonding circuit is the initial step in the completion phase of a wiring job.

(2) Upon completion of the first finishing step, the proper leads to the terminals of switches, ceiling and wall outlets, and fixtures are then installed.

(3) The devices and their cover plates are then attached to the boxes. The fixtures are generally supported by the use of special mounting brackets called fixture studs or hick-eys.

(4) The service-entrance cable and fusing or circuit breaker panels are then connected and the circuits fused.

(5) The final step in the wiring of any building requires the testing of all outlets by the insertion of a test prod or test lamp, the operation of all switches in the building, and the loading of all circuits to insure proper circuiting has been installed.

SECTION III. ELECTRICIAN'S TOOLS AND EQUIPMENT

1-12. Purpose

The electrical apparatus and materials that an electrician is required to install and maintain are different from other building materials. Their installation and maintenance require the use of special handtools. This section describes and illustrates the tools normally used by an Army electrician in interior wiring. For additional information on proper tool usage, refer to standard textbooks.

1-13. Pliers

Pliers are furnished with either uninsulated or insulated handles. Although the insulated handle pliers are always used when working on or near "hot" wires, they must not be considered sufficient protection alone and other precautions must be taken. Long-nose pliers are used for close work in panels or boxes. Wire clippers are used to cut wire to size. One type of wire clippers shown in figure 1-9 has a plastic cushion in the cutting head which grips the clipped

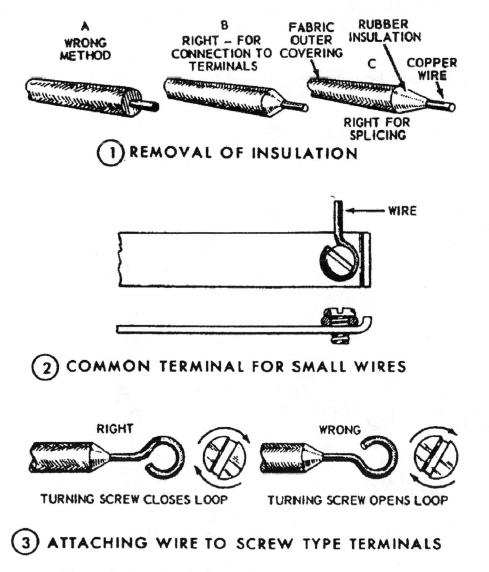

Figure 1-8. Removing insulation and attaching wire to terminals.

wire end and prevents the clipped piece from flying about and injuring personnel. The slip-joint pliers are used to tighten locknuts or small nuts on devices.

1-14. Fuse Puller

The fuse puller shown in figure 1-10 is designed to eliminate the danger of pulling and replacing cartridge fuses by hand. It is also used for bending fuse clips, adjusting loose cutout clips, and handling live electrical parts.

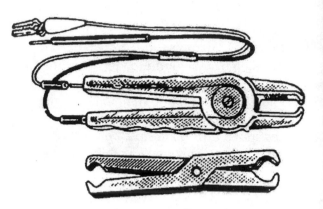

Figure 1-10. Fuse pullers.

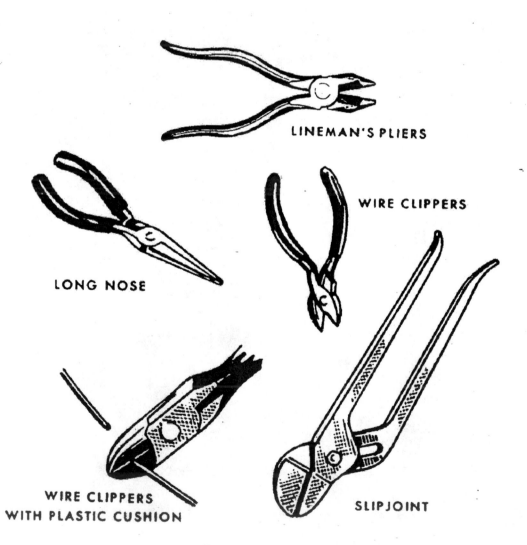

LINEMAN'S PLIERS

WIRE CLIPPERS

LONG NOSE

WIRE CLIPPERS WITH PLASTIC CUSHION

SLIPJOINT

Figure 1-9. Pliers.

The second type of fuse puller, although having the same general configuration, is made of molded plastic. Encased in the handle is an electrical circuit similar to a voltmeter except that the indicating device is a neon glow tube. Test probes are attached to the handle of this fuse puller and may be used to determine if voltage is present in a circuit.

1-15. Screwdrivers

Screwdrivers *(fig. 1-11)* are made in many sizes and tip shapes. Those used by electricians should have insulated handles. Generally the electrician uses screwdrivers in attaching electrical devices to boxes and attaching wires to terminals. One variation of the screwdriver is the screwdriver bit which is held in a brace and used for heavy-duty work. For safe and efficient application, screwdriver tips should be kept square and properly tapered and should be selected to match the screw slot.

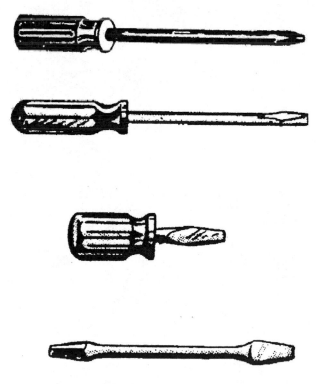

Figure 1-11. Screwdrivers.

1-16. Wrenches

Figure 1-12 shows four types of wrenches used by electricians. Adjustable open-end wrenches, commonly called crescent wrenches, open end, closed end, and socket wrenches are used on hexagonal and square fittings such as machine bolts, hexagon nuts, or conduit unions. Pipe wrenches are used for pipe and conduit work and should not be used where crescent, open end, closed end, or socket wrenches can be used. Their construction will not permit the application of heavy pressure on square **or** hexagonal material, and the continued misuse of the tool in this manner will deform the teeth on the jaw faces and mar the surfaces of the material being worked.

1-17. Soldering Equipment
A standard soldering kit (fig. 1-13) used by electricians consists of nonelectric or electric soldering irons or both, a blowtorch (for heating a nonelectric soldering iron and pipe or wire joints), a spool of solid tin-lead wire solder or flux core solder, and soldering paste. An alcohol or propane torch may also be used in place of the blowtorch. Acid core solder should never be used in electrical wiring.

1-1-8. Drilling Equipment
Drilling equipment (fig. 1-14) consists of a brace, a joist-drilling fixture, an extension bit to allow for drilling into and through deep cavities, an adjustable bit, and a standard wood bit. These are required in electrical work to drill holes in building structures for the passage of conduit or wire in new or modified construction. Similar equipment is required for drilling holes in sheet-metal cabinets and boxes. In this case high speed drills should be used. Carbide drills are used for tile or concrete work. Electric power drills aid in this phase of an electrician's work.

1-19. Woodworking Tools
The crosscut and keyhole saws and wood chisels shown in figure 1-15 are used by electri- cians to remove wooden structural members obstructing a wire or conduit run and to notch studs and joists to take conduit, cable, or box-mounting brackets. They are also used in

13

the construction of wood-panel mounting brackets. The keyhole saw may again be used to cut openings in walls of existing buildings where boxes are to be added.

1-20. Metalworking Tools

The cold chisels and center punches shown in figure 1-16, besides several other types of metalworking tools employed by the electrical trade, are used when working on steel panels. The knockout punch is used either in making or enlarging a hole in a steel cabinet or outlet box. The hacksaw is usually used by an electrician to cut conduit, cable, or wire too large for wire cutters. A light steady stroke of about 40 to 50 times a minute is best. A new blade should always be inserted with the teeth pointing away from the handle. The tension wingnut is tightened until the blade is rigid. Care must be taken because insufficient tension will cause the blade to twist and jam whereas too much tension will caus^c the blade to break. Blades have 14, 18, 24, and 32 teeth per inch. The best blade for general use is one having 18 teeth per inch. A blade with 32 teeth per inch is best for cutting thin material. The mill

CRESCENT

OPEN AND BOX END

PIPE

RATCHET

Figure 1-12. Wrenches.

file shown in the figure is used in filing the sharp ends of cutoffs as a precaution against short circuits.

1-21. Masonry-Working Tools

An electrician should have several sizes of masonry drills in his tool kit. These normally are carbide-tipped and are used to drill holes in brick or concrete walls either for anchoring apparatus with expansion screws or for the passage of conduit or cable. Figure 1-17 shows the carbide-tipped bit used with a power drill and a hand-operated masonry drill.

1-22. Conduit Threaders and Dies
Rigid conduit is normally threaded for installation. Figure 1-18 illustrates one type of con-

duit threader and dies used in cutting pipe threads on conduit. The tapered pipe reamer is used to ream the inside edge of the conduit as a precaution against wire damage. The conduit cutter is used when cutting thin-wall conduit and has a tapered blade attachment for reaming the conduit ends.

1-22. Conduit Threaders and Dies

Rigid conduit is normally threaded for installation. Figure 1-18 illustrates one type of conduit threader and dies used in cutting pipe threads on conduit. The tapered pipe reamer is used to ream the inside edge of the conduit as a precaution against wire damage. The conduit cutter is used when cutting thin-wall conduit

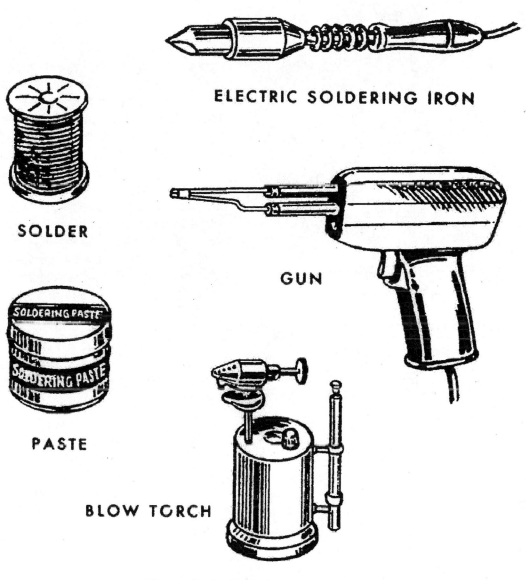

ELECTRIC SOLDERING IRON

SOLDER

GUN

PASTE

BLOW TORCH

Figure 1-13. Soldering equipment.

and has a tapered blade attachment for reaming the conduit ends.

1-23. Knives and Other Insulation-Stripping Tools

Wire and cable insulation is stripped or removed with the tools shown in figure 1-19. The knives and patented wire strippers are used to bare the wire of insulation before making connections. The scissors shown are used to cut insulation and tape. A multipurpose tool designed to cut and skin wires, attach termi-nals, gage wire, and cut small bolts may also be

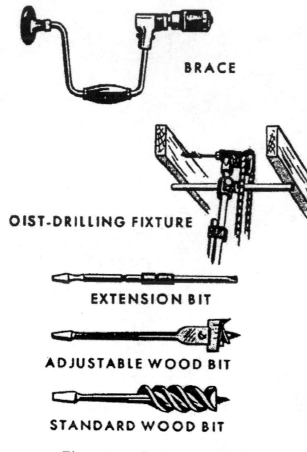

BRACE

OIST-DRILLING FIXTURE

EXTENSION BIT

ADJUSTABLE WOOD BIT

STANDARD WOOD BIT

Figure 1-14. Drilling equipment.

1-24. Hammers
Hammers are used either in combination with other tools such as chisels or in nailing equipment to building supports. Figure 1-20 shows

a carpenter's clawhammer and a machinist's ball peen hammer, both of which can be

advantageously used by electricians in their work.

1-25. Tape
Various types of tapes are used to replace insulation and wire coverings. Friction tape is a cotton tape impregnated with an insulating adhesive compound. It provides weather resistance and limited mechanical protection to a splice already insulated. Rubber or varnished cambric tape may be used as an insulator when replacing wire covering. Plastic electrical tape is made of a plastic material with adhesive on one face. It has replaced friction and rubber tape in the field for 120- and 208-volt circuits, and as it serves a dual purpose in taping joints, it is preferred over the former methods. This is discussed in paragraph 1-9.

1-26. Fish Wire and Drop Chain
a. Fish Wire. Fish wires are used primarily to pull wires through conduits. Many pulls are

16

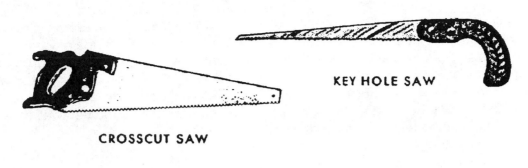

KEY HOLE SAW

CROSSCUT SAW

CHISEL

Figure 1–15. Woodworking tools.

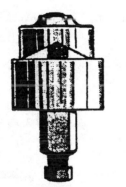

KNOCKOUT PUNCH

HACKSAW AND BLADE

MILL FILE

COLD CHISELS AND PUNCHES

Figure 1–16. Metalworking tools.

quite difficult and require a fish-wire "grip" or "pull" to obtain adequate force on the wire in pulling. The fish wire is made of tempered spring steel about 1/4-inch wide and is available in lengths to suit requirements. It is stiff enough to preclude bending under normal operation but can be pushed or pulled easily around the bends or conduit elbows.

b. Drop Chain. When pulling wires and cables in existing buildings, the electrician will normally employ a fish wire or drop chain between studs. A drop chain consists of small chain links attached to a lead or iron weight. It is used only to feed through wall openings in a vertical plane.

STARR DRILL

POWER-OPERATED

DRILL HOLDING WEDGE

HAND-OPERATED

Figure 1-17. Masonry drills.

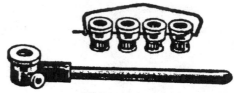

CONDUIT THREADER

CONDUIT REAMER

THIN-WALL CONDUIT CUTTER AND REAMER

Figure 1-18. Conduit threader, reamers, and cutter.

ELECTRICIAN'S KNIFE

ELECTRICIAN'S SCISSORS

SKINNING KNIFE

STRIPPER

MULTIPURPOSE TOOL

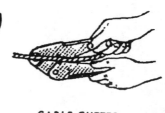

CABLE CUTTER

Figure 1-19. Insulation-stripping tools.

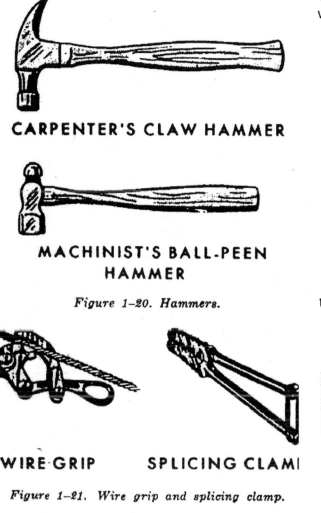

CARPENTER'S CLAW HAMMER

MACHINIST'S BALL-PEEN HAMMER

Figure 1-20. Hammers.

WIRE-GRIP   **SPLICING CLAMI**

Figure 1-21. Wire grip and splicing clamp.

RUBBER-HANDLE GUARDS

Figure 1-22. Extension light (without bulb).

1-27. Ruler and Measuring Tape

As an aid in cutting conduit to exact size as well as in determining the approximate material quantities required for each job, the electrician should be equipped with a folding rule and a steel tape.

1-28. Wire Clamps and Grips

To pull wire through conduit and to pull open-wire installations tight, the wire grip shown in

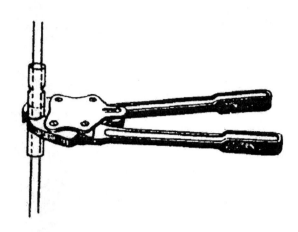

Figure 1-23. Thin-wall conduit impinger.

120 VOLTS (LAMPS DIM)

208 VOLTS (LAMPS BRIGHT)

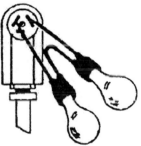

120 OR 208 VOLTS TEST LAMP

FOR 120 VOLT ONLY

Figure 1-24. Test lamps.

figure 1-21 is an invaluable aid. As seen in the figure, the wire grip has been designed so that the harder the pull on the wire, the tighter the wire will be gripped. Also shown in the figure is the splicing clamp used to twist the wire pairs into a uniform and tight joint when making splices.

1-29. Extension Cord and Light

The extension light shown in figure 1-22 normally is supplied with a long extension cord and is used by the electrician when normal building lighting has not been installed or is not functioning.

1-30. Thin-Wall Conduit Impinger

When the electrician uses indenter type couplings and connectors with thin-wall conduit, an indenter tool (a thin-wall conduit impinger shown in fig. 1-23) must be used to attach these fittings permanently to the conduit. This

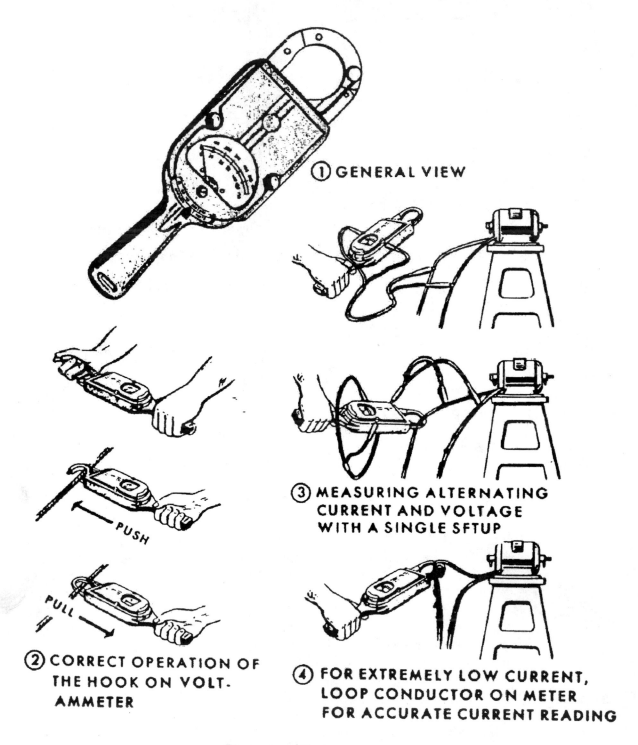

① GENERAL VIEW

② CORRECT OPERATION OF THE HOOK ON VOLT-AMMETER

③ MEASURING ALTERNATING CURRENT AND VOLTAGE WITH A SINGLE SETUP

④ FOR EXTREMELY LOW CURRENT, LOOP CONDUCTOR ON METER FOR ACCURATE CURRENT READING

Figure 1–25. Hook-on volt-ammeter.

tool has points which, when pressed against the fittings, form indentations in the fitting and are pressed into the wall of the tubing to hold it on the conduit. The use of these slip-on fittings and the impinger materially reduces the

installation time required in electrical installations and thus reduces the cost of thin-wall conduit installations considerably.

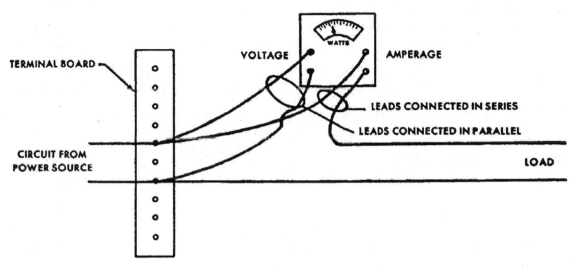

Figure 1-26. Wattmeter connection.

1-31. Wire Code Markers

Tapes with identifying numbers or nomenclature are available for the purpose of permanently identifying wires and equipment. These are particularly valuable to identify wires in complicated wiring circuits, in fuse circuit breaker panels, or in junction boxes.

1-32. Meters and Test Lamps

a. Test Lamps. An indicating voltmeter or test lamp is useful when determining the system voltage or locating the ground lead, and for testing circuit continuity through the power source. They both have a light which glows in the presence of voltage. Figure 1-24 shows a test lamp used as a voltage indicator.

b. Hook-On Volt-Ammeter. A modern method of measuring current flow in a circuit uses the hook-on volt-ammeter (1, fig. 1-25) which does not need to be hooked into the circuit. Two, figure 1-25 shows its ease of operation. To make a measurement, the hook-on section is opened by hand and the meter is placed against the conductor. A

slight push on the handle snaps the section shut; a pull springs the hook on the C-shaped current transformer open and releases the conductor. Applications of this meter are shown in 3, figure 1-25 where voltage is being measured using the meter leads. Current is measured using the hook-on section. With three coils around the meter (4, fig. 1-25) the current reading will be three times the actual current flowing through the wire. To obtain the true current, therefore, this reading is divided by 3. The hook-on volt-ammeter can be used only on alternating current circuits and can measure current only in a single conductor.

c. Wattmeter. The basic unit of measurement for electric power is the watt. In the power ratings of electric devices used by domestic consumers of electricity, the term watts signifies that, when energized at the normal line voltage, the apparatus will use electricity at the specified rate. In alternating-current circuits, power is the product of three quantities: the potential (volt), the current (amperes), and the power factor (percent). Power is measured by a wattmeter (fig. 1-26). This instrument is connected (fig. 1-26) so that the current in the measured circuit flows through the stationary field coils in the wattmeter and the voltage across the measured circuit is impressed upon the wattmeter-armature circuit, which includes movable coils and a fixed resistor. The power factor is automatically included in the measurement because the torque developed in the wattmeter is always proportional to the product of the instantaneous values of current and voltage. Consequently, the instrument gives a true indication of the power, or rate at which energy is being utilized.

SECTION IV. WIRING MATERIALS

1-33. Introduction
There are many different wiring systems currently in use which vary in complexity from the simple-to-install open wiring to the more complex conduit systems. These various systems contain common components. This section describes these common or general use materials.

1-34. Electrical Conductors
a. *Single Conductors.* Electrical conductors that provide the paths for the flow of electric current generally consist of copper or aluminum wire or cable over which an insulating material is formed. The insulating material insures that the path of current flow is through the conductor rather than through extraneous paths, such as conduits, water pipes, and so on. The wires or conductors are initially classified by type of insulation applied and wire gage. The various types of insulation are in turn subdivided according to their maximum operating

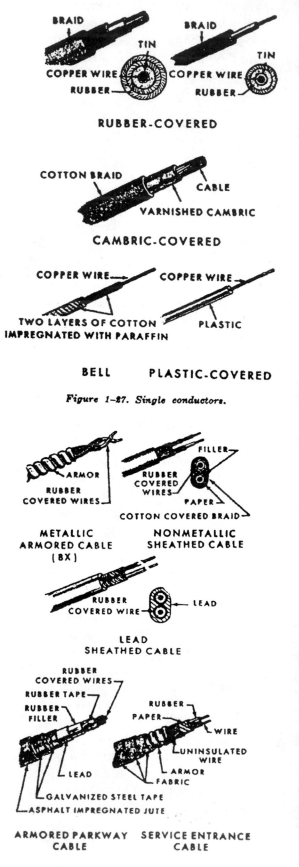

Figure 1-27. Single conductors.

Figure 1-28. Multiconductor cables.

temperatures and nature of use. Figure 1-27 illustrates the more common single conductors used in interior wiring systems. Table C-2 lists the common trade classification of wires and compares them as to type, temperature rating, and recommended use.

b. Wire Sizes. The wire sizes are denoted by the use of the American Wire Gage (AWG) standards. The largest gage size is No. 0000. Wires larger than this are classified in size by their circular mil cross-sectional area. One circular mil is the area of a circle with a diameter of 1/1,000 of an inch. Thus, if a wire has a diameter of 0.10 inch or 100 mil, the cross sectional area is 100 X 100 or 10,000 circular mils. The most common wire sizes used in interior wiring are 14, 12, and 10 and they are usually of solid construction. Some characteristics of the numbering system are

(1) As the numbers become larger, the size of the wire decreases.

(2) The sizes normally used have even numbers, e.g., 14, 12, and 10.

(3) Numbers 8 and 6 wires, which are furnished either solid or stranded, are normally used for heavy-power circuits or as service-entrance leads to buildings. Wire sizes larger than these are used for extremely heavy loads and for poleline distributions.

c. Multiconductor Cables. There are many types of installations of electrical wiring where the use of individual conductors spaced and supported side by side becomes an inefficient as well as hazardous practice. For these installations, multiconductor cables have been designed and manufactured. Multiconductor cables consist of the individual conductors as outlined in *b* above, arranged in groups of two or more. An additional insulating or protective shield is formed or wound around the group of conductors. The individual conductors are color coded for proper identification. Figure 1-28 illustrates some of the types of multiconductors. The description and use of each type are given in (1) through (5) below.

(1) Armored cable, commonly referred to as BX, can be supplied either in two- or three-wire types and with or without a lead sheath. The wires in BX, matched with a bare equipment ground wire, are initially twisted together. This grouping, totaling three or four wires with the ground, is then wrapped in coated paper and a formed self-locking steel armor. The cable without a lead sheath is widely used for interior wiring under dry conditions. The lead sheath is required for installation in wet locations and through masonry or concrete building partitions where added protection for the copper conductor wires is required.

(2) Nonmetallic sheathed cable consists of two or three rubber- or thermoplastic-insulated wires, each covered with a jute type of filler material which acts as a protective insulation against mishandling. This in turn is covered with an impregnated cotton braid. The cable is light in weight, simple to install, and comparatively low priced. It is used quite extensively in interior wiring, but is not approved for use in wet locations. A dual-purpose plastic sheathed cable with solid copper conductors can be used underground outdoors or indoors. It needs no conduit, and its flat shape and gray or ivory color make it ideal for surface wiring. It resists moisture, acid, and corrosion and can be run through masonry or between studding.

(3) Lead-covered cable consists of two or more rubber-covered conductors surrounded by a lead sheathing which has been extruded around it to permit its installation in wet and underground locations. Lead-covered cable can also be immersed in water or installed in areas where the presence of liquid or gaseous vapors would attack the insulation on other types.

(4) Parkway cable provides its own protection from mechanical injury and therefore can be used for underground services by burying it in the ground without any protecting conduit. It normally consists of rub-

ber-insulated conductors enclosed in a lead sheath and covered with a double spiral of galvanized steel tape which acts as a mechanical protection for the lead. On top of the tape, a heavy braid of jute saturated with a waterproofing compound is applied for additional weather protection.

(5) Service-entrance cable normally has three wires with two insulated and braided conductors laid parallel and wound with a bare conductor. Protection against damage for this assembly is obtained by encasing the wires in heavy tape or armor, which serves as an inner cushion, and covering the whole assembly with braid. Though the cable normally serves as a power carrier from the exterior service drop to the service equipment of a building, it may also be used in interior-wiring circuits to supply power to electric ranges and water heaters at voltages not exceeding 150 volts to ground pro

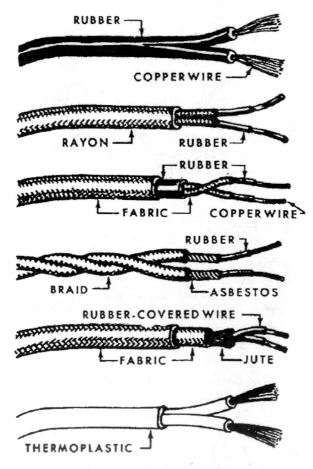

Figure 1-29. Types of flexible cords.

vided the outer covering is armor. It may also be used as a feeder to other buildings on the same premises under the same conditions, if the bare conductor is used as an equipment grounding conductor from a main distribution center located near the main service switch.

d. Cords. Many items using electrical power are either of the pendant, portable, or vibration type. In these cases the use of cords as shown in figure 1-29 is authorized for delivery of power. These can be grouped and designated as either lamp, heater, or heavy-duty power cords. Lamp cords are supplied in many forms. The most common types are the single-paired rubber-insulated and twisted-paired cords. The twisted-paired cords consist of two cotton-wound conductors which have been covered with rubber and rewound with cotton braid. Heater cords are similar to this latter type except that the first winding is replaced by heat-resistant asbestos. Heavy-duty or hard-service cords are normally supplied with two or more conductors surrounded by cotton and rubber insulation. In manufacture, these are first twisted or stranded. The voids created in the twisting process are then filled with jute and the whole assembly covered with rubber. All cords, whether of this type or of the heater or lamp variety, have the conductors color coded for ease of identification. Table C-8 groups by common trade terms the cords found in general use and illustrates some of their characteristics.

1-35. Electrical Boxes

a. Design. Outlet boxes bind together the elements of a conduit or armored cable system in a continuous grounded system. They provide a means of holding the conduit in position, a space for mounting such devices as switches and receptacles, protection for the device, and space for making splices and connections. Outlet boxes are manufactured in either sheet steel, porcelain, bakelite, or cast iron and are either round, square, octagonal, or rectangular. The fabricated steel box is available in a number of different designs. For example, some boxes are of the sectional or "gang" variety, while others have integral brackets for mounting on studs and joists. Moreover, some boxes have been designed to receive special cover plates so that switches, receptacles, or lighting fixtures may be more easily installed. Other designs facilitate installation in plastered surfaces. Regardless of the design or material, they all should have sufficient interior volume to allow for the splicing of conductors or the making of connections. For this reason the allowable minimum depth of outlet boxes is limited to 11/2 inches in all cases except where building-supporting members would have to be cut. In this case the minimum depth can be reduced to 1/2 inch.

b. Selection. The selection of boxes in an electrical system should be made in accordance with tables C-9 and C-10 which list the maximum allowable conductor capacity for each type of box. In these tables a conductor running through the box

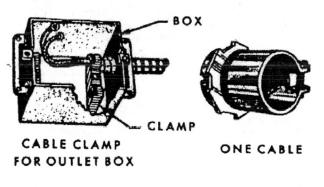

CABLE CLAMP FOR OUTLET BOX

ONE CABLE

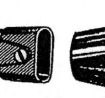

TWO CABLE

ARP-CORNER NE CABLE

ANTISHORT BUSHING

Figure 1-30. Armored-cable fittings.

is counted along with each conductor terminating in the box. For example, one conductor running through a box and two terminating in the box would equal three conductors in the

box. Consequently, any of the boxes listed would be satisfactory. The tables apply for boxes that do not contain receptacles, switches, or similar devices. Each of these items mounted in a box will reduce by one the maximum number of conductors allowable as shown in the tables.

c. Outlet Boxes for Rigid and Thin-Watt Circuit and Armored Cable. Steel or cast iron outlet boxes are generally used with rigid and thin-wall conduit or armored cable. The steel boxes are either zinc- or enamel-coated, the zinc coating being preferred when installing conduit in wet locations. All steel boxes have "knockouts." These knockouts are indentations in the side, top, or back of an outlet box, sized to fit the standard diameters of conduit fittings or cable connectors. They usually can be removed with a small cold chisel or punch to facilitate entry into the box of the conduit or cable. Boxes designed specifically for armored-cable use also have integral screw clamps located in the space immediately inside the knockouts and thus eliminate the need for cable connectors. This reduces the cost and labor of installation. Box covers are normally required when it is necessary to reduce the box openings, provide mounting lugs for electrical devices, or to cover the box when it is to be used as a junction. Figure 1-30 illustrates several types of cable connectors and also a cable clamp for use in clamping armored cable in an outlet box. The antishort bushing shown in the figure is inserted between the wires and the armor to protect the wire from the sharp edges of the cut armor when it is cut with a hacksaw or cable cutter.

d. Outlet Boxes for Nonmetallic Sheathed Cable and Open Wiring.

(1) *Steel.* Steel boxes are also used for nonmetallic cable and open wiring. However, the methods of box entry are different from those for conduit and armored-cable wiring because the electrical conductor wires are not protected by a hard surface. The connectors and interior box clamps used in nonmetallic and open wiring are formed to provide a smooth surface for securing the

cable rather than being the sharp-edged type of closure normally used.

(2) *Nonmetallic.* Nonmetallic outlet boxes made of either porcelain or bakelite may also be used with open or nonmetallic sheathed wiring. Cable or wire entry is generally made by removing the knockouts of preformed weakened blanks in the boxes.

(3) *Special.* In open wiring, conductors should normally be installed in a loom from the last support to the outlet box. Although all of the boxes described in (1) and (2) above are permissible for open wiring, a special loom box is available which has its back corners "sliced off" and allows for loom and wire entry at this sliced-off position.

e. Attachment Devices for Outlet Boxes. Outlet boxes which do not have brackets are supported by wooden cleats or bar hangers as illustrated in figure 1-31.

(1) *Wooden cleats.* Wooden cleats are first cut to size and nailed between two wooden members. The boxes are then either nailed or screwed to these cleats through holes provided in their back plates.

(2) *Strap hangers.* If the outlet box is to be mounted between studs, mounting straps are necessary. The readymade straps are handy
and accommodate not only a single box, but a 2, 3, 4, or 5 gang box.

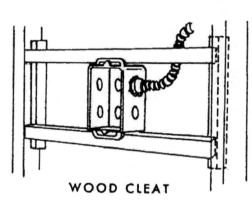

WOOD CLEAT

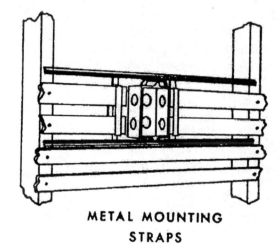

METAL MOUNTING STRAPS

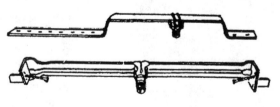

BAR HANGERS

Figure 1-31. Typical box mountings.

(3) *Bar hangers.* Bar hangers are prefabricated to span the normal 16-inch and 24-inch joist and stud spacings and are obtainable for surface or recessed box installation. They are nailed to the joist or stud exposed faces. The supports for recessed boxes normally are called offset bar hangers.

(4) *Patented supports.* When boxes have to be installed in walls that are already plastered, several patented supports can be used for mounting. These obviate the need for installing the boxes on wooden members and thus eliminate extensive chipping and replas-tering.

1-36. Knobs, Tubes, Cleats, Loom, and Special Connectors

Open wiring requires the use of special insulating supports and tubing to insure a safe installation. These supports, called knobs and cleats, are smooth-surfaced and made of porcelain. Knobs and cleats support the wires which are run singly or in pairs on the surface of the joists or studs in the buildings. Tubing or tubes, as they are called, protect the wires from abrasion when passing through wooden members. Insulation of loom of the "slip-on" type is used to cover the wires on box entry and at wire-crossover points. The term "loom" is applied to a continuous flexible tube woven of cambric material impregnated with varnish.

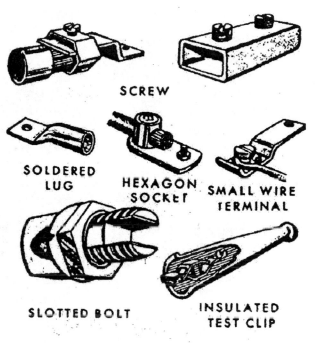

Figure 1-32. Cable and wire connectors.

At points where the type of wiring may change and where boxes are not specifically required, special open wiring to cable or conduit wiring connectors should be used. These connectors are threaded on one side to facilitate connection to a conduit and have holes on the other side to accommodate wire splices but are designed only to carry the wire to the next junction box. The specific methods of installation and use of these items are covered in standard textbooks.

1-37. Cable and Wire Connectors

Code requirements state that "Conductors shall be spliced or joined with splicing devices approved for the use or by brazing, welding, or soldering with a fusible metal or alloy. Soldered splices shall first be so spliced as to be mechanically and electrically secure without solder and then soldered." Soldering or splicing devices are used as added protection because of the ease of wiring and the high quality of connection of these devices. Assurance of high quality is the responsibility of the electrician who selects the proper size of connector relative to the number and size of wires.

27

Figure 1-32 shows some of the many types of cable and wire connectors in common use.

1-38. Straps and Staples

a. *Policy.* All conduits and cables must be attached to the structural members of a building in a manner that will preclude sagging. The cables must be supported at least every 4 1/2 feet for either a vertical or horizontal run and must have a support in the form of a strap or staple within 12 inches of every outlet box. Conduit-support spacings vary with the size and rigidity of the conduit. See table C-11 for support of rigid nonmetallic conduit and paragraph 6-2 for rigid metal conduit.

b. *Cable Staples.* A very simple and effective method of supporting BX cables on wooden members is by the use of cable staples as shown in 1, figure 1-33.

c. *Insulating Staples.* Bell or signal wires

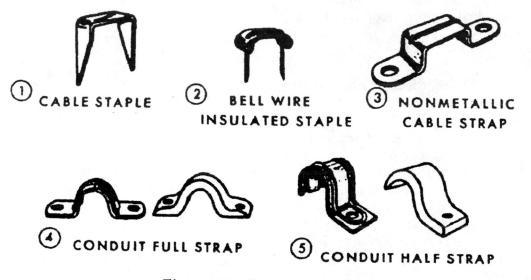

① CABLE STAPLE ② BELL WIRE INSULATED STAPLE ③ NONMETALLIC CABLE STRAP

④ CONDUIT FULL STRAP ⑤ CONDUIT HALF STRAP

Figure 1-33. Straps and staples.

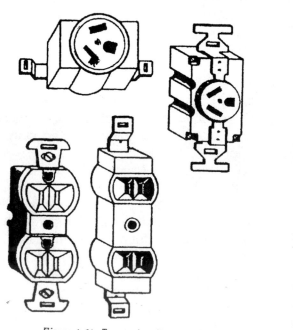

Figure 1-34. Types of wall receptacles.

are normally installed in pairs in signal systems. The operating voltage and energy potential is so low in these installations (12 to 24 volts) that protective coverings such as conduit or loom are not required. To avoid any possibility of shorting in the circuit, they are normally supported on wood joists or studs by insulated staples of the type shown in 1, figure 1-33.

d. *Straps.* Conduit and cable straps (3, 4, and 5, fig. 1-33) are supplied as either one-hole or two-hole supports and are formed to fit the contour of the specific material for which they are designed. The conduit and cable straps are attached to building materials by "anchors" designed to suit each type of supporting material. For example, a strap is attached to a wood stud or joist by nails or screws. Expanding anchors are used for box or strap attachment to cement or brick structures and also to plaster or plaster-substitute surfaces. Toggle and "molly" bolts are used where the surface wall is thin and has a concealed air space which will allow for the release of the toggle or expanding sleeve.

1-39. Receptacles, Fixtures, and Receptacle Covers

a. *Applicability.* Portable appliances and devices are readily connected to an electrical supply circuit by means of an outlet called a receptacle. For interior wiring these outlets are installed either as single or duplex receptacles. Receptacles previously installed, and their replacements in the same box, may be two-wire receptacles. All others must be the three-wire type. The third wire on the three-wire receptacle is used to provide a ground lead to the equipment which receives power from the receptacle. This guards against dangers from current leakage due to faulty insulation or exposed wiring and helps prevent accidental shock. The receptacles are constructed to receive plug prongs either by a straight push action or by a twist-and-turn push action. Fixtures are similar to receptacles but are used to connect the electrical supply circuit directly to lamps inserted in their sockets.

b. *Knob-and-Tube- Wiring.* Receptacles with their entire enclosures made of some insulating material, such as bakelite, may be used without metal outlet boxes for exposed, open wiring or nonmetalli sheathed cable.

c. *Conduit and Cable.* The receptacles (fig. 1-34) commonly used with conduit and cable installations are constructed with yokes to facilitate their installation in outlet boxes. In this case they are attached to the boxes by metal screws through the yokes, threaded into the box. Wire connections are made at the receptacle terminals by screws which are an integral part of the outlet. Receptacle covers made of either brass, steel, or nonmetallic materials are then attached to box and receptacle installations to afford complete closure at the outlets.quick inexpensive electrical wiring installation method since they aie installed on the

wall surface instead of inside the wall (fig. 1-35).

(1) Surface metal raceway is basically of two types: one-piece construction or two-piece construction. When working with the one-piece construction type, the metal raceway is installed like conduit, then the wires are "pulled" to make the necessary electrical connections. If working with the two-piece construction type, the base piece is installed along

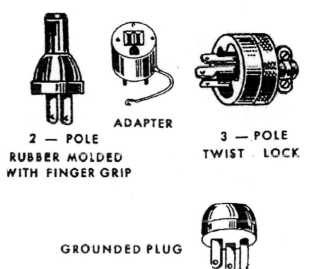

ADAPTER

2 — POLE
RUBBER MOLDED
WITH FINGER GRIP

3 — POLE
TWIST LOCK

GROUNDED PLUG

Figure 1-86. Attachment plugs.

a. *Surface Metal Raceways.* These provide a quick inexpensive electrical wiring installation method since they aie installed on the wall surface instead of inside the wall (fig. 1-35).

1-40. Plugs and Cord Connectors

a. *Plugs.* Portable appliances and devices that are to be connected to receptacles have their electrical cords equipped with plugs (fig. 1-86) that have prongs which mate with the slots in the outlet receptacles. A three-prong

(1) Surface metal raceway is basically of two types: one-piece construction or two-piece construction. When working with the one-piece construction type, the metal raceway is installed like conduit, then the wires are "pulled" to make the necessary electrical

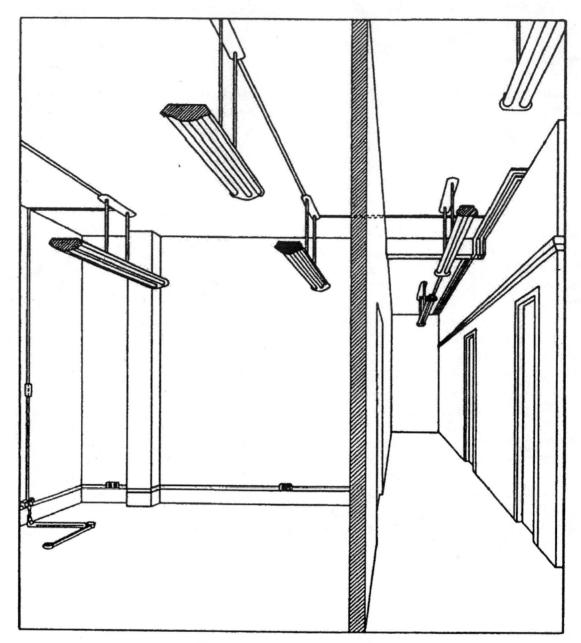

Figure 1-35. Surface metal raceways.

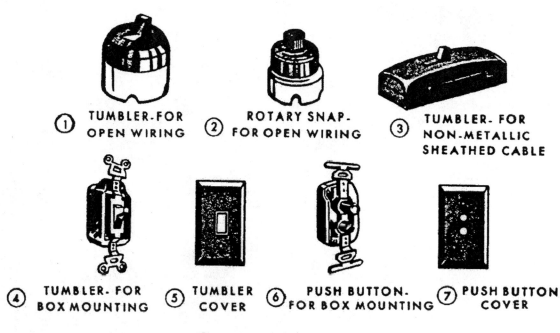

① TUMBLER-FOR OPEN WIRING ② ROTARY SNAP- FOR OPEN WIRING ③ TUMBLER- FOR NON-METALLIC SHEATHED CABLE

④ TUMBLER- FOR BOX MOUNTING ⑤ TUMBLER COVER ⑥ PUSH BUTTON- FOR BOX MOUNTING ⑦ PUSH BUTTON COVER

Figure 1–38. Switches and covers.

connections. If working with the two-piece construction type, the base piece is installed along

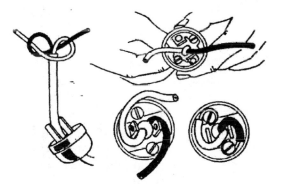

Figure 1–37. The Underwriters knot.

plug can fit into a two-prong receptacle by using an adapter. If the electrical conductors connected to the outlet have a ground system, the lug on the lead wire of the adapter is connected to the center screw holding the receptacle cover to the box. Many of these plugs are permanently molded to the attached cords. There are other types of cord-grips that hold the cord firmly to the plug. Twist-lock plugs have patented prongs that catch and are firmly held to a mating receptacle when the plugs are inserted into the receptacle slots and twisted. Where the plugs do not have cord-grips, the cords should be tied with an Underwriters knot (fig. 1-37) at plug entry to eliminate tension on

the terminal connections when the cord is connected and disconnected from the outlet receptacle. Figure 1-37 shows the steps to be used in tying this type of knot.

b. Cord Connectors. There are some operating conditions where a cord must be connected to a portable receptacle. This type of receptacle, called a cord connector body or a female plug, is attached to the cord in a manner similar to the attachment of the male plug outlined in *a* above.

1-41. Switches and Covers

a. Definition. A switch is a device used to connect and disconnect an electrical circuit from the source of power. Switches may be either one-pole or two-pole for ordinary lighting or receptacle circuits. If they are of the one-pole type, they must be connected to break the hot or ungrounded conductor of the circuit. If of the two-pole type, the hot and ground connection can be connected to either pole on the line side of the switch. Switches are also available that can be operated in combinations of two, three, or more in one circuit. These are called three-way and four-way switches and are discussed fully in paragraph 3-15.

b. Open and Nonmetallic Sheathed Wiring. Switches used for exposed open wiring and nonmetallic sheathed cable wiring are usually of the tumbler type with the switch and cover in one piece. Other less common ones are the rotary-snap and pushbutton types. These switches are generally nonmetallic in composition (1, 2, and 3, fig. 1-38).

c. Conduit and Cable Installations. The tumbler switch and cover plates (4 and 5, fig. 1-38) normally used for outlet-box installation are mounted in a manner similar to that for box type receptacles and covers and are in two pieces. Foreign installations may still use pushbutton switches as shown in 6 and 7, figure 1-38.

d. Entrance Installations. At every power-line entry to a building a switch and fuse combination or circuit breaker switch of a type similar to that shown in figure 1-39 must be installed at the service entrance. This switch must be rated to disconnect the building load while in use at the system voltage. Entrance or service switches, as they are commonly called, consist of one "knife" switch blade for every hot wire of the power supplied. The switch is generally enclosed and sealed in a sheet-steel cabinet. When connecting or disconnecting the building circuit, the blades are operated simultaneously through an exterior handle by the rotation of a common shaft holding the blades. The neutral or grounded conductor is not switched but is connected at a neutral terminal within the box. Many entrance switches are equipped with integral fuse blocks or circuit breakers which protect the building load. The circuit breaker type of entrance switch is preferred, particularly in field installations, because of its ease of resetting after the overload condition in the circuit has been cleared.

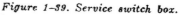

Figure 1-39. Service switch box.

1-42. Fuses and Fuse Boxes

a. Fuses. The device for automatically opening a circuit when the current rises beyond the safety limit is technically called a cutout, but more commonly is called a fuse. All circuits and electrical apparatus must be protected from short circuits or dangerous overcurrent conditions through correctly rated fuses.

(1) *Standard.* The cartridge type fuse is used for current rating above 30 amperes in interior wiring systems. The ordinary plug or screw type fuse is satisfactory for incandescent lighting or heating appliance circuits.

(2) *Special.* On branch circuits, wherever motors are connected, time-lag fuses should be used instead of the standard plug or cartridge type fuse. These fuses have self-compensating elements which maintain and hold the circuit in line during a momentary heavy ampere drain, yet cut out the circuit under normal short-circuit conditions. The heavy ampere demand normally occurs in motor circuits when the motor is started.

Examples of such circuits are the ones used to power oil burners or air conditioners.

b. Fuse Boxes. As a general rule the fusing of circuits is concentrated at centrally located fusing or distribution panels. These panels are normally located at the service-entrance switch in small buildings or installed in several power centers in large buildings. The number of service centers or fuse boxes in the latter case would be determined by the connected power load. Fuses and a fuse box are shown in figure 1-40.

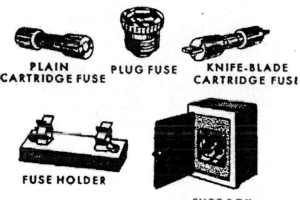

Figure 1-40. Typical fuses and fuse box.

1-43. Circuit Breaker Panels
Circuit breakers are devices resembling switches that trip or cut out the circuit in case of overamperage. They perform the same function as fuses and can be obtained with time-lag opening features similar to the special fuses outlined in paragraph 1-42. Based on their operation, they may be classified as a thermal, magnetic, or combination thermal-magnetic reaction type. A thermal type circuit breaker has a bimetallic element integrally built within the breaker that responds only to fluctuations in temperature within the circuit. The element is made by bonding together two strips of dissimilar metal, each of which has a different coefficient of expansion. When a current is flowing in the circuit, the heat created by the resistance of the bimetallic element will expand each metal at a different rate causing the strip to bend. The element acts as a latch in the circuit as the breaker mechanism is adjusted so that the element bends just far enough under a specified current to trip the breaker and open the circuit. A magnetic circuit breaker responds to changes in the magnitude of current flow. In operation an increased current flow will create enough magnetic force to "pull up" an armature, opening the circuit. The motor circuits for closer adjustment to motor rating while the circuit conductors are protected, as usual, by another circuit breaker. The thermal-magnetic breaker, as the name implies, combines the features of the thermal and magnetic types. Practically all of the

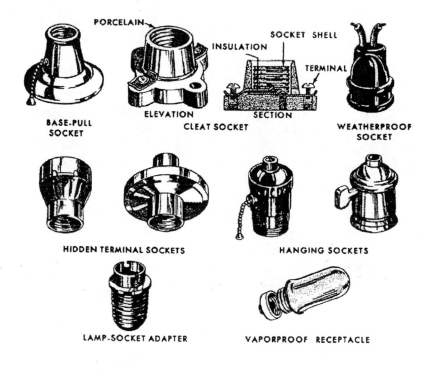

molded case magnetic circuit breaker is usually used in

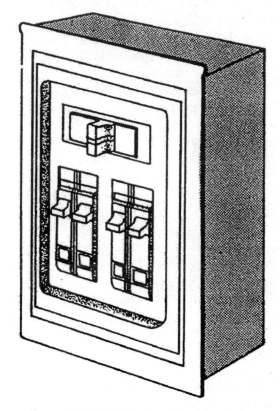

Figure 1–41. Typical circuit breaker box.

circuit breakers used in lighting panelboards are of this type. The thermal element protects against overcurrents in the lower range and the magnetic element prof- .ts against the higher range usually occurri.ig from short circuits. During the last decade, circuit breakers have been used to a greater extent than fuses because they can be manually reset after tripping, whereas fuses require replacement. Fuses may easily be replaced with higher capacity ones that do not protect the circuit. This is difficult to do with circuit breakers. In addition they combine the functions of fuse and switch, and when tripped by overloads or short circuits, all of the ungrounded conductors of a circuit are opened simultaneously. Each branch circuit must have a fuse or circuit breaker protecting each ungrounded conductor. Some installations may or may not have a main breaker that disconnects everything. As a guide during installation, if it does not require more than six movements of the hand to open

all the branch circuit breakers, a main breaker or switch is not required ahead of the branch-circuit breaker. However, if more than six movements of the hand are required, a separate disconnecting main circuit breaker is required ahead of the branch-circuit breaker. Each 120-volt circuit requires a single-pole (one-pole) breaker which has its own handle. Each 208-volt circuit requires a double-pole (two-pole) breaker to protect both ungrounded conductors. You can, however, place two single-pole breakers side by side, and tie the two handles together mechanically to give double-pole protection. Both handles can then be moved by a single movement of the hand. A two-pole breaker may have one handle or two handles which are mechanically tied together, but either one requires only one movement of the hand to break the circuit. Figure 1-41 illustrates a typical circuit breaker panel.

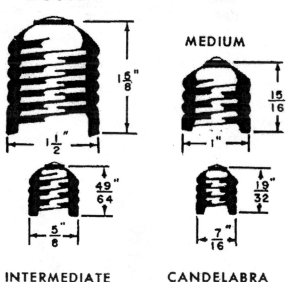

Figure 1–43. General lamp-socket sizes.

BELL

SIREN

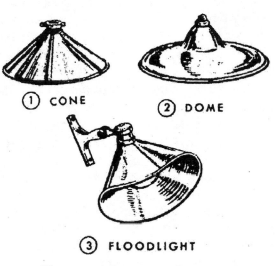

BUZZER

Figure 1-44 Types of signal equipment.

1-44. Lampholders and Sockets

Lamp sockets as shown in figure 1-42 are generally screw-base units placed in circuits as holders for incandescent lamps. A special type of lampholder has contacts, rather than a screw base, which engage and hold the prongs of fluorescent lamps when they are rotated in the holder. The sockets can generally be attached to a hanging cord or mounted directly on a wall or ceiling in open wiring installations by using screws or nails in the mounting holes provided in the nonconducting material which is molded or formed around the lamp socket. The two mounting holes in a procelain lamp socket are spaced so the sockets may also be attached to outlet box "ears" or a plaster ring with machine screws. The screw threads molded or rolled in the ends of the lampholder sockets also facilitate their ready integration in other types of lighting fixtures such as table lamps, floor lamps, or hanging fixtures which have reflectors or decorative shades. In an emergency, a socket may also be used as a receptacle. The socket is converted to a receptacle by screwing in a female plug. One type of ceiling lampholder has a grounded outlet located on the side. Lamp sockets are produced in many different sizes

and shapes. A few of the most common sizes are shown in figure 1-43.

① CONE ② DOME

③ FLOODLIGHT

Figure 1-45. Types of reflectors.

1-45. Signal Equipment
Figure 1-44 illustrates the most common components in interior wiring signal systems.

1-45. Signal Equipment

Figure 1-44 illustrates the most common components in interior wiring signal systems. Their normal operating voltages are 6, 12, 18, or 24 volts, ac or dc. As a general rule they are connected by open-wiring methods and are used as interoffice or building-to-building signal systems.

1-46. Reflectors and Shades

Figure 1-45 shows several types of reflectors and shades which are used to focus the lighting effect of bulbs. Of these, some are used to flood an area with high intensity light and are called floodlights. Others, called spotlights, concentrate the useful light on a small area. Both floodlights and spotlights can come in two- or three-light clusters with swivel holders. They can be mounted on walls or posts or on spikes pushed into the ground. One and two, figure 1-45 illustrate reflectors that deliver normal building light of average intensity in a pattern similar to the floodlight shown in 3, figure 1-45.

1-47. Incandescent Lamps

The most common light source for general use is the incandescent lamp. Though it is the least efficient type of light, its use is preferred over the fluorescent type because of its low initial cost, ease of maintenance, convenience, and flexibility. Its flexibility and convenience is readily seen by the wide selection of wattage ratings that can be inserted in one type socket. Further, since its emitted candlepower is directly proportional to the voltage, a lower voltage application will dim the light. A high rated voltage application from a power source will increase its intensity. Although an incandescent light is economical, it is also inefficient because a large amount of the energy supplied to it is converted to heat rather than light. Moreover, it does not give a true light because the tungsten filament emits a great deal more red and yellow light than does the light of the sun. Incandescent lamps are shown in figure 1-46. Incandescent lights are normally built to last 1,000 hours when operating at their rated voltage.

1-48. Fluorescent Lamps

Fluorescent lamps (fig. 1-47) are either of the conventional "hot cathode" or "cold cathode" type. The "hot cathode" lamp has a coiled wire type of electrode, which when heated gives off electrons. These electrons collide with mercury

Figure 1-46. Incandescent lamps.

atoms, provided by mercury vapor in the tubes, which produces ultraviolet radiation. Fluorescent powder coatings on the inner walls of the tubes absorb this radiation and transform the energy into visible light. The "cold cathode" lamp operates in a similar manner except that its electrode consists of a cylindrical tube. It receives its name because the heat is generated over a larger area and, therefore, the cathode does not reach as high a temperature as in the "hot cathode" tube. The "cold cathode" is less efficient but has a longer operating life than the "hot cathode" unit. It is used most frequently on flashing circuits. Because of the higher light output per watt input, more illumination and less heat is obtained per watt from fluorescent lamps than from incandescent ones. Light diffusion is also better, and surface brightness is lower. The life of fluorescent lamps is also longer compared to filament types. However, the fluorescent lamp, because of its design, cannot control its beam of light as well as the incandescent type and has a tendency to produce stroboscopic effects which are counteracted by phasing arrangements. Moreover, when voltage fluctuations are severe, the lamps may go out prematurely or start slowly. Finally, the higher initial cost in fluorescent lighting, which requires auxiliary equipment such as starters, ballasts, special landholders, and fixtures (fig. 1-47), is also a disadvantage compared with other types of illumination.

a. *Construction.* The fluorescent lamp is an electric discharge lamp that consists of an elongated tubular bulb with an oxide-coated filament sealed in each end to comprise two electrodes (fig. 1-48). The bulb contains a drop of mercury and a small amount of argon gas. The inside surface of the bulb is coated with a fluorescent phosphor. The lamp produces invisible, short wave (ultraviolet) radiation by the discharge through the mercury vapor in the bulb. The phosphor absorbs the invisible radiant energy and reradiates it over a band of wavelengths that are sensitive to the eye.

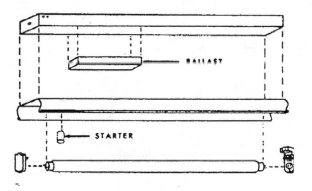

Figure 1-47. Fluorescent light accessories.

(1) Detail illumination is required where the intensity of general illumination is not sufficient, and in engineering spaces for examination of gages. The fixtures for detail illumination commonly use single fluorescent lamps. One and two, figure 1-48, illustrates the wiring arrangement for these single units, and three, figure 1-48, shows a multiple unit.

(2) Because of greater cost and shorter life of 8-watt fluorescent lamps, as compared to 15-watt and 20-watt lamps, fixtures with 8-watt lamps are used only for detail illumination and general illumination within locations where space is restricted.

(3) Although the fluorescent lamp is basically an ac lamp, it can be operated on dc with the proper auxiliary equipment. The current is controlled by an external resistance in series with the lamp (4, fig. 1-48). Since there is no voltage peak, starting is

more difficult and thermal switch starters are required. The lamp tends to deteriorate at one end due to the uniform direction of the current. This may he par-tially overcome by reversing the lamp position or the direction of current periodically.

(4) Because of the power lost in the resistance ballast box in the dc system, the overall lumens per watt efficiency of the dc system is about 60 percent of the ac system. Also, lamps operated on dc may provide as little as 80 percent of rated life.

(5) The fluorescent lamp, like all discharge light sources, requires special auxiliary control equipment for starting and stabilizing the lamp. This equipment consists of an iron-core choke coil, or ballast, and an automatic starting switch connected in series with the lamp filaments. The starter (starting switch) can be either a glow switch or a thermal switch. A resistor must be connected in series with the ballast in dc circuits because the ballast alone does not offer sufficient resistance to maintain the arc current steady.

(6) Each lamp must be provided with an individual ballast and starting switch, but the auxiliaries for two lamps are usually enclosed in a single container.. The auxiliaries for fluorescent lighting fixtures are mounted inside the fixture above the reflector. The starting switches (starters) project through the reflector so that they can be replaced readily. The circuit diagram for the fixture appears on the ballast container.

b. *Operation.* A fluorescent lamp equipped with a glow-switch starter is illustrated in 1, figure 1-48. The glow-switch starter is essentially a glow lamp containing neon or argon gas and two metallic electrodes. One electrode has a fixed contact, and the other electrode is a U-shaped, bimetal strip having a movable contact. These contacts are normally open.

(1) When the circuit switch is closed, there is practically no voltage drop across the ballast, and the voltage across the starter, S, is sufficient to produce a plow around the bimetallic strip in the glow lamp.

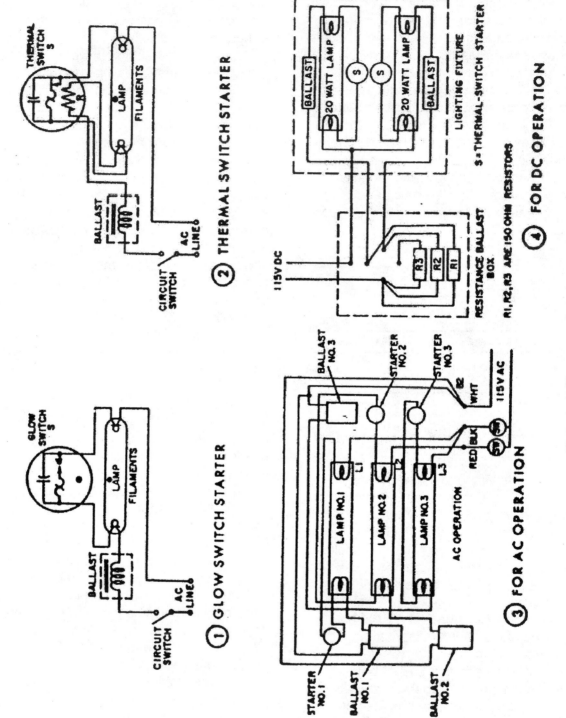

Figure 1-68. Fluorescent schematic.

The heat from the glow causes the bimetal   strip to distort and touch the fixed electrode.

This action shorts out the glow discharge and the bimetal strip starts to cool as the starting circuit of the fluorescent lamp is completed. The starting current flows through the lamp filament in each end of the fluorescent tube, causing the mercury to vaporize. Current does not flow across the lamp between the electrodes at this time because the path is short circuited by the starter and because the gas in the bulb is nonconducting when the electrodes are cold. The preheating of the fluorescent tube continues until the bimetal strip in the starter cools sufficiently to open the starting circuit.

(2) When the starting circuit opens, the decrease of current in the ballast produces an induced voltage across the lamp electrodes. The magnitude of this voltage is sufficient to ionize the mercury vapor and start the lamp. The resulting glow discharge (arc) through the fluorescent lamp produces a large amount of ultraviolet radiation that impinges on the phosphor, causing it to fluoresce and emit a relatively bright light. During normal operation the voltage across the fluorescent lamp is not sufficient to produce a glow in the starter. Hence, the contacts remain open and the starter consumes no energy.

(3) A fluorescent lamp equipped with a thermal-switch starter is illustrated in 1, figure 1-48. The thermal-switch starter consists of two normally closed metallic contacts and a series resistance contained in a cylindrical enclosure. One contact is fixed, and the movable contact is mounted on a bimetal strip.

(4) When the circuit switch is closed, the starting circuit of the fluorescent lamp is completed (through the series resistance, R) to allow the preheating current to flow through the electrodes. The current through the series resistance produces heat that causes the bimetal strip to bend and open the starting circuit. The accompanying induced voltage produced by the ballast starts the lamp. The normal operating current holds the thermal switch open.

(5) The majority of thermal-switch starters use some energy during normal operation of the lamp. However, this switch insures more positive starting by providing an adequate preheating period and a higher induced starting voltage.

c. Characteristics. The failure of a hot-cathode fluorescent lamp usually results from loss of electron-emissive material from the electrodes. This loss proceeds gradually throughout the life of the lamp and is accelerated by frequent starting. The rated average life of the lamp is based on normal burning periods of 3 to 4 hours. Blackening of the ends of the bulb progresses gradually throughout the life of the lamp.

(1) The efficiency of the energy conversion of a fluorescent lamp is very sensitive to changes in temperature of the bulb. The maximum efficiency occurs in the range of 100° F. to 120° F., which is the operating temperature that corresponds to an ambient room temperature range of 65° to 85° F. The efficiency decreases slowly as the temperature is increased above normal, but also decreases very rapidly as the temperature is decreased below normal. Hence, the fluorescent lamp is not satisfactory for locations in which it will be subjected to wide variations in temperature. The reduction in efficiency with low ambient room temperature can be minimized by operating the fluorescent lamp in a tubular glass enclosure so that the lamp will operate at more nearly the desired temperature.

(2) Fluorescent lamps are relatively efficient compared with incandescent lamps. For example, a 40-watt fluorescent lamp produces approximately 2800 lumens, or 70 lumens per watt. A 40-watt fluorescent lamp produces six times as much light per watt as does the comparable incandescent lamp.

(3) Fluorescent lamps should be operated at voltage within 8 percent of their rated voltage. If the lamps are operated at lower voltages, uncertain starting may result, and if operated at higher voltages, the ballast may overheat. Operation of the lamps at either lower or higher voltages results in decreased lamp life. The characteristic

curves for hot-cathode fluorescent lamps show the effect of variations from rated voltage on the condition of lamp operation. Also, the performance of fluorescent lamps depends to a great extent on the characteristics of the ballast, which determines the power delivered to the lamp for a given line voltage.

(4) When lamps are operated on ac circuits, the light output executes cyclic pulsations as the current passes through zero. This reduction in light output produces a flicker that is more noticeable in fluorescent lamps than in incandescent lamps at frequencies of 50 and 60 cycles and may cause unpleasant stro-boscopic effects when moving objects are viewed. The cyclic flicker can be minimized by combining two or three lamps in a fixture and operating the lamps on different phases of a three-phase system. Where only single-phase circuits are available, leading current may be supplied to one lamp and lagging current to another through a lead-lag ballast circuit so that the light pulsations compensate each other.

(5) The fluorescent lamp is inherently a high power-factor device, but the ballast required to stabilize the arc is a low power-factor device. The voltage drop across the ballast is usually equal to the drop across the arc, and the resulting power factor for a single-lamp circuit with ballast is about 50 percent. The low power factor can be corrected in a single-lamp ballast circuit by a capacitor shunted across the line. This correction is accomplished in a two-lamp circuit by means of a "tulamp" auxiliary that connects a capacitor in series with one of the lamps to displace the lamp currents, and, at the same time, to remove the unpleasant stroboscopic effects when moving objects come into view.

d. Glow Lamps. Glow lamps are electric discharge light sources, which are used as indicator or pilot lights for various instruments and on control panels. These lamps have relatively low light output, and thus are used to indicate when circuits are energized or to indicate the operation of electrical equipment installed in remote locations.

(1) The glow lamp consists of two closely spaced metallic electrodes sealed in a glass bulb that contains an inert gas. The color of the light emitted by the lamp depends on the gas. Neon gas produces a blue light. The lamp must be operated in series with a current-limiting device to stabilize the discharge. This current-limiting device consists of a high resistance that is usually contained in the lamp base.

(2) The glow lamp produces light only when the voltage exceeds a certain striking voltage. As the voltage is decreased somewhat below this value, the glow suddenly vanishes. When the lamp is operated on alternating current, light is produced only during a portion of each half cycle, and both electrodes are alternately surrounded with a glow. When the lamp is operated on direct current, light is produced continuously, and only the negative electrode is surrounded with a glow. This characteristic makes it possible to use the glow lamp as an

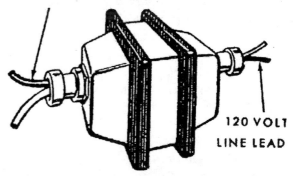

Figure 1-49. Transformer.

indicator of alternating current and direct current. It has the advantages of small size, ruggedness, long life, and negligible current consumption, and can be operated on standard lighting circuits.

1-49. Transformers
The transformer is a device for changing alternating current voltages into either high voltages for efficient powerline transmission or low voltages for consumption in lamps, electrical

devices, and machines. Transformers vary in size according to their power handling rating. Their selection is determined by input and output voltage and load current requirements. For example, the transformer used to furnish power for a doorbell reduces 115-volt alternating current to about 6 to 10 volts. This is accomplished by two primary wire leads which are permanently connected to the 115-volt circuit and two secondary screw terminals from the low voltage side of the transformer. Figure 1-49 shows a common type of signal system transformer. It is used to lower the building voltage of 120 volts or 240 volts ac to the 6, 12,

18, or 24 volts ac. The wires shown are input and output leads. In figure 1-49 the input leads are smaller than the output leads because the current in the output circuit is greater than in the input circuit.

1-50. Rotating Equipment

Generally, lighting circuits outnumber motor or power circuits in every installation.

However, the energy consumption of motors and power loads is probably greater than the lighting-circuit consumption. The electrician should study in order to further his knowledge of motors, motor controls, their maintenance and repair.

APPENDIX
ELECTRIC DATA

Table C-1. Characteristics of Electrical Systems

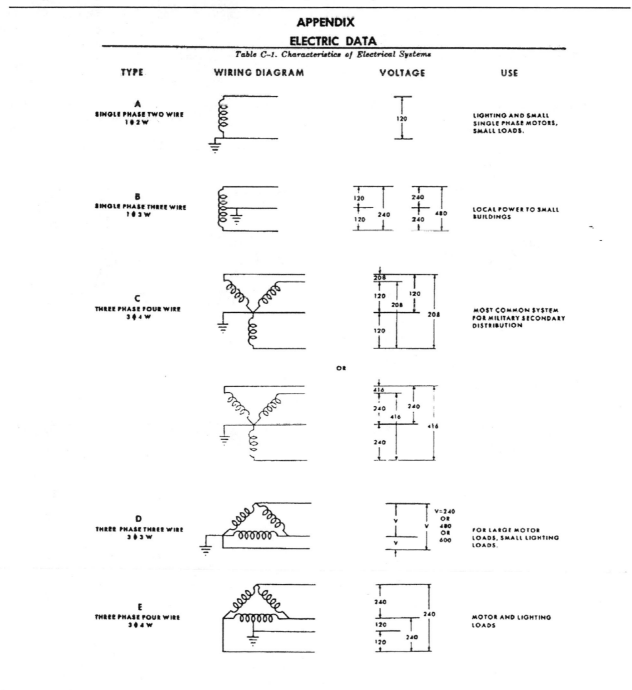

Table C-2. Conductor Insulation

Trade Name	Type Letter	Temp. rating	Application Provisions
Rubber-Covered Fixture Wire	*RF-1	60°C 140°F	Fixture wiring. Limited to 300 V.
Solid or 7-Strand	*RF-2	60°C 140°F	Fixture wiring.
Rubber-Covered Fixture Wire	*FF-1	60°C 140°F	Fixture wiring. Limited to 300 V.
Flexible Stranding	*FF-2	60°C 140°F	Fixture wiring.
Heat-Resistant Rubber-Covered Fixture Wire	*RFH-1	75°C 167°F	Fixture wiring. Limited to 300 V.
Solid or 7-Strand	*RFH-2	75°C 167°F	Fixture wiring.
Heat-Resistant Rubber-Covered Fixture Wire	*FFH-1	75°C 167°F	Fixture wiring. Limited to 300 V.
Flexible Stranding	*FFH-2	75°C 167°F	Fixture wiring.
Thermoplastic-Covered Fixture Wire—Solid or Stranded	*TF	60°C 140°F	Fixture wiring.
Thermoplastic-Covered Fixture Wire—Flexible Stranding	*TFF	60°C 140°F	Fixture wiring.
Cotton-Covered, Heat-Resistant, Fixture Wire	*CF	90°C 194°F	Fixture wiring. Limited to 300 V.
Asbestos-Covered Heat-Resistant, Fixture Wire	*AF	150°C 302°F	Fixture wiring. Limited to 300 V. and Indoor Dry Location.
Silicone Rubber Insulated Fixture Wire	*SF-1	200°C 392°F	Fixture wiring. Limited to 300 V.
Solid or 7 Strand	*SF-2	200°C 392°F	Fixture wiring
Silicone Rubber Insulated Fixture Wire	*SFF-1	150°C 302°F	Fixture wiring. Limited to 300 V.
Flexible Stranding	*SFF-2	150°C 302°F	Fixture wiring.
Code Rubber	R	60°C 140°F	Dry locations.
Heat-Resistant Rubber	RH	75°C 167°F	Dry locations.
Heat Resistant Rubber	RHH	90°C 194°F	Dry locations.
Moisture-Resistant Rubber	RW	60°C 140°F	Dry and wet locations. For over 2000 volts, insulation shall be ozone-resistant.
Moisture and Heat Resistant Rubber	RH-RW	60°C 140°F	Dry and wet locations. For over 2000 volts, insulation shall be ozone-resistant.

*Fixture wires are not intended for installation as branch circuit conductors nor for the connection of portable or stationary appliances.

ELECTRICAL TERMS AND FORMULAS

CONTENTS

ELECTRICAL TERMS AND FORMULAS

Terms

AGONIC.--An imaginary line of the earth's surface passing through points where the magnetic declination is 0°; that is, points where the compass points to true north.

AMMETER.--An instrument for measuring the amount of electron flow in amperes.

AMPERE.-- The basic unit of electrical current.

AMPERE-TURN.--The magnetizing force produced by a current of one ampere flowing through a coil of one turn.

AMPLIDYNE.--A rotary magnetic or dynamo-electric amplifier used in servomechanism and control applications.

AMPLIFICATION.--The process of increasing the strength (current, power, or voltage) of a signal.

AMPLIFIER.--A device used to increase the signal voltage, current, or power, generally composed of a vacuum tube and associated circuit called a stage. It may contain several stages in order to obtain a desired gain.

AMPLITUDE.--The maximum instantaneous value of an alternating voltage or current, measured in either the positive or negative direction.

ARC.--A flash caused by an electric current ionizing a gas or vapor.

ARMATURE.--The rotating part of an electric motor or generator. The moving part of a relay or vibrator.

ATTENUATOR.--A network of resistors used to reduce voltage, current, or power delivered to a load.

AUTOTRANSFORMER.--A transformer in which the primary and secondary are connected together in one winding.

BATTERY.--Two or more primary or secondary cells connected together electrically. The term does not apply to a single cell.

BREAKER POINTS.--Metal contacts that open and close a circuit at timed intervals.

BRIDGE CIRCUIT.--The electrical bridge circuit is a term referring to any one of a variety of electric circuit networks, one branch of which, the "bridge" proper, connects two points of equal potential and hence carries no current when the circuit is properly adjusted or balanced.

BRUSH.--The conducting material, usually a block of carbon, bearing against the commutator or sliprings through which the current flows in or out.

BUS BAR.--A primary power distribution point connected to the main power source.

CAPACITOR.--Two electrodes or sets of electrodes in the form of plates, separated from each other by an insulating material called the dielectric.

CHOKE COIL.--A coil of low ohmic resistance and high impedance to alternating current.

CIRCUIT.--The complete path of an electric current.

CIRCUIT BREAKER.--An electromagnetic or thermal device that opens a circuit when the current in the circuit exceeds a predetermined amount. Circuit breakers can be reset.

CIRCULAR MIL.--An area equal to that of a circle with a diameter of 0.001 inch. It is used for measuring the cross section of wires.

COAXIAL CABLE.--A transmission line consisting of two conductors concentric with and insulated from each other.

COMMUTATOR.--The copper segments on the armature of a motor or generator. It is cylindrical in shape and is used to pass power into or from the brushes. It is a switching device.

CONDUCTANCE.--The ability of a material to conduct or carry an electric current. It is the reciprocal of the resistance of the material, and is expressed in mhos.

CONDUCTIVITY.--The ease with which a substance transmits electricity.

CONDUCTOR.--Any material suitable for carrying electric current.

CORE.--A magnetic material that affords an easy path for magnetic flux lines in a coil.

COUNTER E.M.F.--Counter electromotive force; an e.m.f. induced in a coil or armature that opposes the applied voltage.

CURRENT LIMITER.--A protective device similar to a fuse, usually used in high amperage circuits.

CYCLE.--One complete positive and one complete negative alternation of a current or voltage.

DIELECTRIC.--An insulator; a term that refers to the insulating material between the plates of a capacitor.

1

DIODE.—Vacuum tube—a two element tube that contains a cathode and plate; semiconductor —a material of either germanium or silicon that is manufactured to allow current to flow in only one direction. Diodes are used as rectifiers and detectors.

DIRECT CURRENT.—An electric current that flows in one direction only.

EDDY CURRENT.—Induced circulating currents in a conducting material that are caused by a varying magnetic field.

EFFICIENCY.—The ratio of output power to input power, generally expressed as a percentage.

ELECTROLYTE.—A solution of a substance which is capable of conducting electricity. An electrolyte may be in the form of either a liquid or a paste.

ELECTROMAGNET.—A magnet made by passing current through a coil of wire wound on a soft iron core.

ELECTROMOTIVE FORCE (e.m.f.).—The force that produces an electric current in a circuit.

ELECTRON.—A negatively charged particle of matter.

ENERGY.—The ability or capacity to do work.

FARAD.—The unit of capacitance.

FEEDBACK.—A transfer of energy from the output circuit of a device back to its input.

FIELD.—The space containing electric or magnetic lines of force.

FIELD WINDING.—The coil used to provide the magnetizing force in motors and generators.

FLUX FIELD.—All electric or magnetic lines of force in a given region.

FREE ELECTRONS.—Electrons which are loosely held and consequently tend to move at random among the atoms of the material.

FREQUENCY.—The number of complete cycles per second existing in any form of wave motion; such as the number of cycles per second of an alternating current.

FULL-WAVE RECTIFIER CIRCUIT.—A circuit which utilizes both the positive and the negative alternations of an alternating current to produce a direct current.

FUSE.—A protective device inserted in series with a circuit. It contains a metal that will melt or break when current is increased beyond a specific value for a definite period of time.

GAIN.—The ratio of the output power, voltage, or current to the input power, voltage, or current, respectively.

GALVANOMETER.—An instrument used to measure small d-c currents.

GENERATOR.—A machine that converts mechanical energy into electrical energy.

GROUND.—A metallic connection with the earth to establish ground potential. Also, a common return to a point of zero potential. The chassis of a receiver or a transmitter sometimes the common return, and therefore the ground of the unit.

HENRY.—The basic unit of inductance.

HORSEPOWER.—The English unit of power equal to work done at the rate of 550 foot pounds per second. Equal to 746 watts electrical power.

HYSTERESIS.—A lagging of the magnetic flux in a magnetic material behind the magnetizing force which is producing it.

IMPEDANCE.—The total opposition offered the flow of an alternating current. It may consist of any combination of resistance, inductive reactance, and capacitive reactance.

INDUCTANCE.—The property of a circuit which tends to oppose a change in the existing current.

INDUCTION.—The act or process of producing voltage by the relative motion of a magnetic field across a conductor.

INDUCTIVE REACTANCE.—The opposition the flow of alternating or pulsating current caused by the inductance of a circuit. It measured in ohms.

INPHASE.—Applied to the condition that exists when two waves of the same frequency pass through their maximum and minimum values of like polarity at the same instant.

INVERSELY.—Inverted or reversed in position or relationship.

ISOGONIC LINE.—An imaginary line drawn through points on the earth's surface where the magnetic deviation is equal.

JOULE.—A unit of energy or work. A joule energy is liberated by one ampere flowing for one second through a resistance of one ohm.

KILO.—A prefix meaning 1,000.

LAG.—The amount one wave is behind another in time; expressed in electrical degrees.

LAMINATED CORE.—A core built up from thin sheets of metal and used in transformers and relays.

LEAD.—The opposite of LAG. Also, a wire connection.

LINE OF FORCE.—A line in an electric or magnetic field that shows the direction of the force.

LOAD.—The power that is being delivered by any power producing device. The equipment that uses the power from the power producing device.

MAGNETIC AMPLIFIER.—A saturable reactor type device that is used in a circuit to amplify or control.

MAGNETIC CIRCUIT.—The complete path of magnetic lines of force.

MAGNETIC FIELD.—The space in which a magnetic force exists.

MAGNETIC FLUX.—The total number of lines of force issuing from a pole of a magnet.

MAGNETIZE.—To convert a material into a magnet by causing the molecules to rearrange.

MAGNETO.—A generator which produces alternating current and has a permanent magnet as its field.

MEGGER.—A test instrument used to measure insulation resistance and other high resistances. It is a portable hand operated d-c generator used as an ohmmeter.

MEGOHM.—A million ohms.

MICRO.—A prefix meaning one-millionth.

MILLI.—A prefix meaning one-thousandth.

MILLIAMMETER.—An ammeter that measures current in thousandths of an ampere.

MOTOR-GENERATOR.—A motor and a generator with a common shaft used to convert line voltages to other voltages or frequencies.

MUTUAL INDUCTANCE.—A circuit property existing when the relative position of two inductors causes the magnetic lines of force from one to link with the turns of the other.

NEGATIVE CHARGE.—The electrical charge carried by a body which has an excess of electrons.

NEUTRON.—A particle having the weight of a proton but carrying no electric charge. It is located in the nucleus of an atom.

NUCLEUS.—The central part of an atom that is mainly comprised of protons and neutrons. It is the part of the atom that has the most mass.

NULL.—Zero.

OHM.—The unit of electrical resistance.

OHMMETER.—An instrument for directly measuring resistance in ohms.

OVERLOAD.—A load greater than the rated load of an electrical device.

PERMALLOY.—An alloy of nickel and iron having an abnormally high magnetic permeability.

PERMEABILITY.—A measure of the ease with which magnetic lines of force can flow through a material as compared to air.

PHASE DIFFERENCE.—The time in electrical degrees by which one wave leads or lags another.

POLARITY.—The character of having magnetic poles, or electric charges.

POLE.—The section of a magnet where the flux lines are concentrated; also where they enter and leave the magnet. An electrode of a battery.

POLYPHASE.—A circuit that utilizes more than one phase of alternating current.

POSITIVE CHARGE.—The electrical charge carried by a body which has become deficient in electrons.

POTENTIAL.—The amount of charge held by a body as compared to another point or body. Usually measured in volts.

POTENTIOMETER.—A variable voltage divider; a resistor which has a variable contact arm so that any portion of the potential applied between its ends may be selected.

POWER.—The rate of doing work or the rate of expending energy. The unit of electrical power is the watt.

POWER FACTOR.—The ratio of the actual power of an alternating or pulsating current, as measured by a wattmeter, to the apparent power, as indicated by ammeter and voltmeter readings. The power factor of an inductor, capacitor, or insulator is an expression of their losses.

PRIME MOVER.—The source of mechanical power used to drive the rotor of a generator.

PROTON.—A positively charged particle in the nucleus of an atom.

RATIO.—The value obtained by dividing one number by another, indicating their relative proportions.

REACTANCE.—The opposition offered to the flow of an alternating current by the inductance, capacitance, or both, in any circuit.

RECTIFIERS.—Devices used to change alternating current to unidirectional current. These may be vacuum tubes, semiconductors such as germanium and silicon, and dry-disk rectifiers such as selenium and copper-oxide.

RELAY.—An electromechanical switching device that can be used as a remote control.

RELUCTANCE.—A measure of the opposition that a material offers to magnetic lines of force.

RESISTANCE.—The opposition to the flow of current caused by the nature and physical dimensions of a conductor.

RESISTOR.—A circuit element whose chief characteristic is resistance; used to oppose the flow of current.

RETENTIVITY.—The measure of the ability of a material to hold its magnetism.

RHEOSTAT.—A variable resistor.

SATURABLE REACTOR.—A control device that uses a small d-c current to control a large a-c current by controlling core flux density.

SATURATION.—The condition existing in any circuit when an increase in the driving signal produces no further change in the resultant effect.

SELF-INDUCTION.—The process by which a circuit induces an e.m.f. into itself by its own magnetic field.

SERIES-WOUND.—A motor or generator in which the armature is wired in series with the field winding.

SERVO.—A device used to convert a small movement into one of greater movement or force.

SERVOMECHANISM.—A closed-loop system that produces a force to position an object in accordance with the information that originates at the input.

SOLENOID.—An electromagnetic coil that contains a movable plunger.

SPACE CHARGE.—The cloud of electrons existing in the space between the cathode and plate in a vacuum tube, formed by the electrons emitted from the cathode in excess of those immediately attracted to the plate.

SPECIFIC GRAVITY—The ratio between the density of a substance and that of pure water, at a given temperature.

SYNCHROSCOPE—An instrument used to indicate a difference in frequency between two a-c sources.

SYNCHRO SYSTEM.—An electrical system t... gives remote indications or control means of self-synchronizing motors.

TACHOMETER.—An instrument for indicati... revolutions per minute.

TERTIARY WINDING.—A third winding on transformer or magnetic amplifier that used as a second control winding.

THERMISTOR.—A resistor that is used compensate for temperature variations in circuit.

THERMOCOUPLE.—A junction of two dissimil... metals that produces a voltage when heate...

TORQUE.—The turning effort or twist which shaft sustains when transmitting power.

TRANSFORMER.—A device composed of two more coils, linked by magnetic lines force, used to transfer energy from o... circuit to another.

TRANSMISSION LINES.—Any conductor ... system of conductors used to carry electric energy from its source to a load.

VARS.—Abbreviation for volt-ampere, reactiv...

VECTOR.—A line used to represent both dire... tion and magnitude.

VOLT.—The unit of electrical potential.

VOLTMETER.—An instrument designed ... measure a difference in electrical potentia... in volts.

WATT.—The unit of electrical power.

WATTMETER.—An instrument for measurin... electrical power in watts.

Formulas

Ohm's Law for d-c Circuits

$$I = \frac{E}{R} = \frac{P}{E} = \sqrt{\frac{P}{R}}$$

$$R = \frac{E}{I} = \frac{P}{I^2} = \frac{E^2}{P}$$

$$E = IR = \frac{P}{I} = \sqrt{PR}$$

$$P = EI = \frac{E^2}{R} = I^2R$$

Resistors in Series

$$R_T = R_1 + R_2 \ldots$$

Resistors in Parallel
Two resistors

$$R_T = \frac{R_1 R_2}{R_1 + R_2}$$

More than two

$$\frac{1}{R_T} = \frac{1}{R_1} + \frac{1}{R_2} + \frac{1}{R_3}$$

ELECTRICAL TERMS AND FORMULAS

R-L Circuit Time Constant equals

$$\frac{L \text{ (in henrys)}}{R \text{ (in ohms)}} = t \text{ (in seconds), or}$$

$$\frac{L \text{ (in microhenrys)}}{R \text{ (in ohms)}} = t \text{ (in microseconds)}$$

R-C Circuit Time Constant equals

R (ohms) X C (farads) = t (seconds)

R (megohms) x C (microfarads) = t (seconds)

R (ohms) x C (microfarads) = t (microseconds)

R (megohms) x C (micromicrofrads = t (microseconds)

Comparison of Units in Electric and Magnetic Circuits.

	Electric circuit	Magnetic circuit
Force	Volt, E or e.m.f.	Gilberts, F, or m.m.f.
Flow	Ampere, I	Flux, Φ, in maxwells
Opposition	Ohms, R	Reluctance, R
Law	Ohm's law, $I = \frac{E}{R}$	Rowland's law $\Phi = \frac{F}{R}$
Intensity of force	Volts per cm. of length	$H = \frac{1.257IN}{L}$, gilberts per centimeter of length
Density	Current density— for example, amperes per cm^2.	Flux density—for example, lines per cm^2., or gausses

Capacitors in Series
Two capacitors

$$C_T = \frac{C_1 C_2}{C_1 + C_2}$$

More than two

$$\frac{1}{C_T} = \frac{1}{C_1} + \frac{1}{C_2} + \frac{1}{C_3} \cdots$$

Capacitors in Parallel

$$C_T = C_1 + C_2 \ldots$$

Capacitive Reactance

$$X_c = \frac{1}{2\pi f C}$$

Impedance in an R-C Circuit (Series)

$$Z = \sqrt{R^2 + X_c^2}$$

Inductors in Series

$$L_T = L_1 + L_2 \ldots \text{(No coupling between coils)}$$

Inductors in Parallel
Two inductors

$$L_T = \frac{L_1 L_2}{L_1 + L_2} \text{ (No coupling between coils)}$$

More than two

$$\frac{1}{L_T} = \frac{1}{L_1} + \frac{1}{L_2} + \frac{1}{L_3} \ldots \text{(No coupling between coils)}$$

Inductive Reactance

$$X_L = 2\pi f L$$

Q of a Coil

$$Q = \frac{X_L}{R}$$

Impedance of an R-L Circuit (series)

$$Z = \sqrt{R^2 + X_L^2}$$

Impedance with R, C, and L in Series

$$Z = \sqrt{R^2 + (X_L - X_C)^2}$$

Parallel Circuit Impedance

$$Z = \frac{Z_1 Z_2}{Z_1 + Z_2}$$

Sine-Wave Voltage Relationships
Average value

$$E_{ave} = \frac{2}{\pi} \times E_{max} = 0.637 E_{max}$$

Effective or r.m.s. value

$$E_{eff} = \frac{E_{max}}{\sqrt{2}} = \frac{E_{max}}{1.414} = 0.707E_{max} = 1.11E_{ave}$$

Maximum value

$$E_{max} = \sqrt{2}E_{eff} = 1.414E_{eff} = 1.57E_{ave}$$

Voltage in an a-c circuit

$$E = IZ = \frac{P}{I \times P.F.}$$

Current in an a-c circuit

$$I = \frac{E}{Z} = \frac{P}{E \times P.F.}$$

Power in A-C Circuit
Apparent power = EI
True power

$$P = EI \cos \theta = EI \times P.F.$$

Power factor

$$P.F. = \frac{P}{EI} = \cos \theta$$

$$\cos \theta = \frac{\text{true power}}{\text{apparent power}}$$

Transformers
Voltage relationship

$$\frac{E}{E} = \frac{N}{N} \quad \text{or} \quad E = E \times \frac{N}{N}$$

Current relationship

$$\frac{I_p}{I_s} = \frac{N_s}{N_p}$$

Induced voltage

$$E_{eff} = 4.44\,BAfN\,10^{-8}$$

Turns ratio equals

$$\frac{N_p}{N_s} = \sqrt{\frac{Z_p}{Z_s}}$$

Secondary current

$$I_s = I_p \frac{N_p}{N_s}$$

Secondary voltage

$$E_s = E_p \frac{N_s}{N_p}$$

Three Phase Voltage and Current Relationshi
With wye connected windings

$$E_{line} = 1.732E_{coil} = \sqrt{3}E_{coil}$$

$$I_{line} = I_{coil}$$

With delta connected windings

$$E_{line} = E_{coil}$$

$$I_{line} = 1.732I_{coil}$$

With wye or delta connected winding

$$P_{coil} = E_{coil}I_{coil}$$

$$P_t = 3P_{coil}$$

$$P_t = 1.732E_{line}I_{line}$$

(To convert to true power multiply by cos

Synchronous Speed of Motor

$$r.p.m. = \frac{120 \times \text{frequency}}{\text{number of poles}}$$

GREEK ALPHABET

Name	Capital	Lower Case	Designates
Alpha	A	α	Angles.
Beta	B	β	Angles, flux density.
Gamma . . .	Γ	γ	Conductivity.
Delta	Δ	δ	Variation of a quantity, increment.
Epsilon . . .	E	ϵ	Base of natural logarithms (2.71828).
Zeta	Z	ζ	Impedance, coefficients, coordinates.
Eta	H	η	Hysteresis coefficient, efficiency, magnetizing force.
Theta	Θ	θ	Phase angle.
Iota	I	ι	
Kappa	K	κ	Dielectric constant, coupling coefficient, susceptibility.
Lambda . . .	Λ	λ	Wavelength.
Mu	M	μ	Permeability, micro, amplification factor.
Nu	N	ν	Reluctivity.
Xi	Ξ	ξ	
Omicron . . .	O	o	
Pi	Π	π	3.1416
Rho	P	ρ	Resistivity.
Sigma	Σ	σ	
Tau	T	τ	Time constant, time-phase displacement.
Upsilon . . .	Υ	υ	
Phi	Φ	φ	Angles, magnetic flux.
Chi	X	χ	
Psi	Ψ	ψ	Dielectric flux, phase difference.
Omega	Ω	ω	Ohms (capital), angular velocity ($2\pi f$).

COMMON ABBREVIATIONS AND LETTER SYMBOLS

Term	Abbreviation or Symbol
alternating current (noun)	a,c.
alternating-current (adj.)	a-c
ampere	a.
area	A
audiofrequency (noun)	AF
audiofrequency (adj.)	A-F
capacitance	C
capacitive reactance	X_c
centimeter	cm.
conductance	G
coulomb	Q
counterelectromotive force	c.e.m.f.
current (d-c or r.m.s. value)	I
current (instantaneous value)	i
cycles per second	c.p.s.
dielectric constant	K,k
difference in potential (d-c or r.m.s. value)	E
difference in potential (instantaneous value)	e
direct current (noun)	d.c.
direct-current (adj.)	d-c
electromotive force	e.m.f.
frequency	f
henry	h.
horsepower	hp.
impedance	Z
inductance	L
inductive reactance	X_L
kilovolt	kv.
kilovolt-ampere	kv.-a.
kilowatt	kw.
kilowatt-hour	kw.-hr.
magnetic field intensity	H
magnetomotive force	m.m.f.
megohm	M
microampere	μ a.
microfarad	μ f.
microhenry	μ h.
micromicrofarad	$\mu\mu$ f.
microvolt	μ v.
milliampere	ma.
millihenry	mh.
milliwatt	mw.
mutual inductance	M
power	P
resistance	R
revolutions per minute	r.p.m.
root mean square	r.m.s.
time	t
torque	T
volt	v.
watt	w.

ANSWER SHEET

TEST NO. ______________ PART ______ TITLE OF POSITION ______________________________
(AS GIVEN IN EXAMINATION ANNOUNCEMENT - INCLUDE OPTION, IF ANY)

PLACE OF EXAMINATION ______________________ (CITY OR TOWN) ______________ (STATE) DATE ______________

RATING

USE THE SPECIAL PENCIL. MAKE GLOSSY BLACK MARKS.

1 A B C D E	26 A B C D E	51 A B C D E	76 A B C D E	101 A B C D E
2 A B C D E	27 A B C D E	52 A B C D E	77 A B C D E	102 A B C D E
3 A B C D E	28 A B C D E	53 A B C D E	78 A B C D E	103 A B C D E
4 A B C D E	29 A B C D E	54 A B C D E	79 A B C D E	104 A B C D E
5 A B C D E	30 A B C D E	55 A B C D E	80 A B C D E	105 A B C D E
6 A B C D E	31 A B C D E	56 A B C D E	81 A B C D E	106 A B C D E
7 A B C D E	32 A B C D E	57 A B C D E	82 A B C D E	107 A B C D E
8 A B C D E	33 A B C D E	58 A B C D E	83 A B C D E	108 A B C D E
9 A B C D E	34 A B C D E	59 A B C D E	84 A B C D E	109 A B C D E
10 A B C D E	35 A B C D E	60 A B C D E	85 A B C D E	110 A B C D E

Make only ONE mark for each answer. Additional and stray marks may be counted as mistakes. In making corrections, erase errors COMPLETELY.

11 A B C D E	36 A B C D E	61 A B C D E	86 A B C D E	111 A B C D E
12 A B C D E	37 A B C D E	62 A B C D E	87 A B C D E	112 A B C D E
13 A B C D E	38 A B C D E	63 A B C D E	88 A B C D E	113 A B C D E
14 A B C D E	39 A B C D E	64 A B C D E	89 A B C D E	114 A B C D E
15 A B C D E	40 A B C D E	65 A B C D E	90 A B C D E	115 A B C D E
16 A B C D E	41 A B C D E	66 A B C D E	91 A B C D E	116 A B C D E
17 A B C D E	42 A B C D E	67 A B C D E	92 A B C D E	117 A B C D E
18 A B C D E	43 A B C D E	68 A B C D E	93 A B C D E	118 A B C D E
19 A B C D E	44 A B C D E	69 A B C D E	94 A B C D E	119 A B C D E
20 A B C D E	45 A B C D E	70 A B C D E	95 A B C D E	120 A B C D E
21 A B C D E	46 A B C D E	71 A B C D E	96 A B C D E	121 A B C D E
22 A B C D E	47 A B C D E	72 A B C D E	97 A B C D E	122 A B C D E
23 A B C D E	48 A B C D E	73 A B C D E	98 A B C D E	123 A B C D E
24 A B C D E	49 A B C D E	74 A B C D E	99 A B C D E	124 A B C D E
25 A B C D E	50 A B C D E	75 A B C D E	100 A B C D E	125 A B C D E

ANSWER SHEET

TEST NO. ______________ PART ______ TITLE OF POSITION ______________________________
(AS GIVEN IN EXAMINATION ANNOUNCEMENT - INCLUDE OPTION, IF ANY)

PLACE OF EXAMINATION ______________________________ ______________________________ DATE ______
(CITY OR TOWN) (STATE)

RATING

USE THE SPECIAL PENCIL. MAKE GLOSSY BLACK MARKS.

1 A B C D E	26 A B C D E	51 A B C D E	76 A B C D E	101 A B C D E
2 A B C D E	27 A B C D E	52 A B C D E	77 A B C D E	102 A B C D E
3 A B C D E	28 A B C D E	53 A B C D E	78 A B C D E	103 A B C D E
4 A B C D E	29 A B C D E	54 A B C D E	79 A B C D E	104 A B C D E
5 A B C D E	30 A B C D E	55 A B C D E	80 A B C D E	105 A B C D E
6 A B C D E	31 A B C D E	56 A B C D E	81 A B C D E	106 A B C D E
7 A B C D E	32 A B C D E	57 A B C D E	82 A B C D E	107 A B C D E
8 A B C D E	33 A B C D E	58 A B C D E	83 A B C D E	108 A B C D E
9 A B C D E	34 A B C D E	59 A B C D E	84 A B C D E	109 A B C D E
10 A B C D E	35 A B C D E	60 A B C D E	85 A B C D E	110 A B C D E

Make only ONE mark for each answer. Additional and stray marks may be counted as mistakes. In making corrections, erase errors COMPLETELY.

11 A B C D E	36 A B C D E	61 A B C D E	86 A B C D E	111 A B C D E
12 A B C D E	37 A B C D E	62 A B C D E	87 A B C D E	112 A B C D E
13 A B C D E	38 A B C D E	63 A B C D E	88 A B C D E	113 A B C D E
14 A B C D E	39 A B C D E	64 A B C D E	89 A B C D E	114 A B C D E
15 A B C D E	40 A B C D E	65 A B C D E	90 A B C D E	115 A B C D E
16 A B C D E	41 A B C D E	66 A B C D E	91 A B C D E	116 A B C D E
17 A B C D E	42 A B C D E	67 A B C D E	92 A B C D E	117 A B C D E
18 A B C D E	43 A B C D E	68 A B C D E	93 A B C D E	118 A B C D E
19 A B C D E	44 A B C D E	69 A B C D E	94 A B C D E	119 A B C D E
20 A B C D E	45 A B C D E	70 A B C D E	95 A B C D E	120 A B C D E
21 A B C D E	46 A B C D E	71 A B C D E	96 A B C D E	121 A B C D E
22 A B C D E	47 A B C D E	72 A B C D E	97 A B C D E	122 A B C D E
23 A B C D E	48 A B C D E	73 A B C D E	98 A B C D E	123 A B C D E
24 A B C D E	49 A B C D E	74 A B C D E	99 A B C D E	124 A B C D E
25 A B C D E	50 A B C D E	75 A B C D E	100 A B C D E	125 A B C D E